ENDANGERED SPECIES

The marmot, hunted for its soft, warm fur, is a fairly sociable animal that lives in a den.

After eating, it perches on high ground to spot intruders and whistle a warning.

PAGE 1

Lowland gorillas such as this one at the San Diego Wild

Animal Park are high-profile animals that visitors come to see.

Uakaris are bald monkeys that live in Peru, Brazil, Ecuador, Colombia

and Venezuela. The three species do not overlap one another's range.

PAGE 4-5

There are large numbers of elephants remaining, but they are considered endangered because of the constant threat of poaching and the human pressures exerted on their habitat.

An impala wanders through Serengeti National Park in Tanzania.

The cheetah uses its long tail for balance and keeps its head motionless when chasing prey; this keeps it in sight. The ancient Egyptians kept cheetahs as pets.

The beautiful St. Lucia parrot has been the victim of hunters

and the destruction of its West Indian habitat.

ENDANGERED SPECIES

GALLERY BOOKS

An Imprint of W. H. Smith Publishers Inc.

112 Madison Avenue New York NY 10016

THE IMAGE BANK

111 Fifth Avenue New York NY 10003

First published in 1988 in New York by Gallery
Books, an imprint of W.H. Smith Publishers Inc.,
112 Madison Avenue, New York, N.Y. 10016

ISBN 0-8317-7118-6

For rights information about the photographs in
this book please contact:

The Image Bank
111 Fifth Avenue, New York, N.Y. 10003

Manufactured in Hong Kong

Produced by Robert M. Tod
Art Direction and Design by Mark Weinberg
Written by Joseph P. Griffith
Edited by Sheila Buff
Editorial Coordination by Elizabeth Loonan
Photo Editing by George DuBose
Editorial Assistance by Ann-Louise Lipman
Assistant Art Direction by Dana Shimizu

The animal shall not be measured by man. In a world older and more complete than ours they move finished and complete, gifted with extensions of the senses we have lost or never attained, living by voices we shall never hear. They are not brethren, they are not underlings; they are other nations, caught with ourselves in the net of life and time, fellow prisoners of the splendor and travail of the earth.

—HENRY BESTON

Suppose someone knocked on the door of your home one day and told you to get out because the land was about to be turned into a parking lot.

You'd probably be upset and angry and would try to call the police or a lawyer and make plans to fight it. This kind of thing just doesn't happen, you'd say. Then suppose that while you were on the phone you heard a noise and suddenly the living room wall came crashing in, leveled by a bulldozer. You'd have no choice but to flee for your life. Then while you were on the street, watching what was left of your home being demolished, a few people passed by and you tried to ask them for help, but they just keep walking. Nobody cared. Then think of all the people who depend on you—your family, your friends. Think of how their lives would be affected by the effect this has on you.

We don't have to carry on this nightmarish analogy for you to understand the plight of endangered species, but let's transfer it to their realm and extend it for a minute. Say that a certain small bug who lives in the forest is a real troublemaker. He's always stealing somebody else's food, he's dirty and spreads germs and if he were a human he'd probably play his radio too loudly. Nobody likes him, least of all humans, so they decide to eradicate him with an insecticide. Then everyone's happy. Everyone except a particular beetle who relied on this bug for food. Now she's hungry because he's scarce. On top of that she's misunderstood; people are always thinking she's "just another bug" and they want to get rid of her too. They don't seem to mind that she doesn't have enough to eat, and soon she's not around either.

That's fine as far as they're concerned, only now there's this group of frogs that ate the beetle that ate the bug. They have to look elsewhere for food, and they're not finding it. They can't adapt. Oh, yes, we forgot to mention that that bug pollinated a few flowers in his time. They're dying out too. Meanwhile the frogs are scarce, which means that a certain unnamed bird is setting a lean table. On top of that, she hasn't been able to raise any young lately. The eggshells are thinner than they used to be and keep breaking. She's heard through the grapevine that that happens as a result of pesticide use, but she thought that affected only pests. She's not a pest. Now that big bird that used to come around all the time, he's a pest. But she hasn't seen him lately . . .

You get the picture. the biosphere of Earth is a finely tuned symbiotic relationship, an interaction between all its creatures and their habitat. The elimination of one, no matter how small, has dire consequences for the others, in ways that may not be felt until it is too late. Many organizations, governments and their agencies are working to reverse the decline of species, but politics, private interests and lawbreakers too often have the upper hand and dictate how the environment is managed. This is illustrated by this book's numerous descriptions of animals, some beautiful and some not, that have been driven to the brink of extinction by hunters seeking their fur or flesh, by land developers eager to turn their habitats into large real-estate projects, or by otherwise well-meaning people who did not know they were causing harm. By not saving animals and the environment man will inevitably doom himself; the fate of the ultimate predator is inextricably linked with that of his prey.

At the time of this writing there were more than 800 animals worldwide on the endangered and threatened species list published by the U.S. Fish and Wildlife Service. Endangered species face more immediate danger than threatened ones. The list is revised about once a year as animals are added or removed because of recovery or extinction. Two species are among the latest casualties—the Amistad gambusia, a small fish found in Texas, and the dusky seaside sparrow, which inhabited Florida marshes—while the American alligator has recovered to the point of being removed from the list.

Environmentalists say the service does not act quickly enought to protect species through addition to the list, and that 300 became extinct in 20 years while the agency tried to decide whether to add them.

Animals and plants are protected under the Endangered Species Act of 1973, which makes it illegal to place flora or fauna in danger of extinction. Among other things it forbids land development, hunting or commercial exploitation that would place any species in that danger. Where it has not actually prevented such activities it has at least made them complicated, costly or overly litigious. It also is charged with developing recovery plans to save species, although it has done so for only a fraction of the number. Meanwhile several thousand species are waiting for evaluation and the necessary paperwork. The act's purpose, according to one Fish and Wildlife official, has not been to oppose development or industries or favor particular species, but to establish and maintain the theory that all forms of life, no matter how small, are worth saving.

The act was up for renewal at the end of 1987, having technically expired, but faced great debate in Congress. Besides the usual political and financial squabbles, some biologists and state officials think the act is doing too good a job, allowing species like bears and wolves to recover and destroy cattle. They argue that where federally protected animals are overpopulated, hunting or reduction of their numbers should be allowed. It is ironic and symbolic that the Fish and Wildlife Service's Office of Endangered Species has itself become extinct, having been reorganized into another division. Critics say this action indicates a widespread attitude about such matters and will hinder the service's ability to deal with them.

There are many private organizations worldwide concerned about the plight of animals and actively working to save them. Most of them have no real power except as lobbyists, but they raise money and awareness to supplement the work of governments and their agencies. Their methods may be controversial, such as when the organization GreenPeace directly confronted whaling boats and the French government's nuclear testing program, the latter with loss of human life. More often they are economic efforts such as boycotts and lobbying to protest commercial exploitation of animals or the destruction of their habitats, or scientific programs of study, conservation and rescue.

The World Wildife Fund is one of the foremost organizations, with branches in most countries. It collects money from many sources and funds many conservation programs. Some of the efforts it has made to rescue or recover various species are outlined in this book.

The Fund works closely with the International Union for the Conservation of Nature and Natural Resources. The IUCN was formed in 1948 in conjunction with the United Nations Education, Scientific and Cultural Organization (UNESCO). It brought together under one umbrella for one purpose various governments, conservation organizations and scientists. One of its major projects has been the publication of Red Data Books, which provide detailed information about species and the threats they face. It also monitors trade in them. Through the IUCN's efforts, the Convention on Trade in Endangered Species (CITES) has been signed by about 90 countries. In signing it governments pledge to prohibit trade in such species, although the law is enforced with varying degrees of conviction. CITES is merely an agreement by which the countries pledge to be bound; IUCN has no enforcement powers.

UNESCO adopted the International Convention for the Protection of the World Cultural and Natural Heritage, or World Heritage Convention, in 1972. Its purpose was to safeguard the cultural and natural heritage of mankind in various areas of the world, including national parks and archeological landmarks. Besides artistic and cultural treasures like the Taj Mahal, the Acropolis and the Pyramids, some of the places on the World Heritage List are wildlife areas like Australia's Great Barrier Reef and Kakadu National Park, Tanzania's Serengeti National Park and Ngorongoro Conservation Area, the U.S. Grand Canyon and Everglades national parks, and Ecuador's Galapagos Islands. The organization's Man and Biosphere Program studies and attempts to improve the complex relationship between people and the environment. Its biosphere reserves are a worldwide network involved in conserving and managing the environment. It sponsors symposiums on and study of such areas as Sub-Saharan Africa, coastal and inland waterways, and tropical forests.

The African Wildlife Foundation has concentrated on saving the wild animals of that continent. Typical projects have included the continuation of the work of the late Dian Fossey with the mountain gorillas of Rwanda, surveys of Tanzania's reserves and national parks and attempts to control the illegal trade in rhino horns. Among its programs are education plans and clubs to teach the youth of Africa to appreciate and conserve their natural resources.

The Audubon Society is North America's oldest conservation organization, founded in 1905 and named after the bird artist John James Audubon. It monitors and publicizes all aspects of the environment and conservation. It publishes a monthly magazine and a large annual report on the state of wildlife.

Nature reserves are one method by which endangered species are protected. Where public access is permitted, they attract thousands of tourists each year, bringing in much-needed revenue, creating jobs, and raising public consciousness about environmental issues. The dramatic intensity of large animals pulls visitors into zoos and whale-watch cruises, and the receipts help organizations maintain more obscure species. But unless such programs are effectively managed they can also have an adverse effect on the environment, as when offroad vehicles that transport tourists significantly damage the soil and terrain of game parks. The cure sometimes becomes worse than the disease.

Captive breeding is another protective strategy. Some animals, like the giant panda, do not breed well to begin with, and even less so in captivity, while others, like crocodilians, fare much better. Some large birds, like bald eagles and whooping cranes, lay two eggs, but one seems to be merely insurance. The siblings fight for supremacy in the nest and only one lives. This is being dealt with by removing one egg and placing it in the nest of another compatible species, where the chick can survive and mature.

Many factors hinder the efforts to protect animals. There is a widespread belief that people should be helping other people, not animals, especially where humans are suffering, such as in areas of war, famine or drought. What is overlooked is the above-mentioned symbiotic relationship and the many opportunities for humans to benefit from animals without killing them, such as by developing new food sources or studying them to gain clues about survival and environmental adaptation.

Access to remote or warring areas containing the animals' habitats is often denied, so study cannot take place, or governments are unwilling or unable to cooperate for various reasons. When animals are studied there is often great disparity in reported information and research methods. This is why Latin names are used for scientific identification; they are universally recognized, while the common names vary greatly from place to place.

Politics is usually a big stumbling block. Guidelines for study or protection are sometimes ignored because they are created by competing organizations that want credit or control. In listing species as endangered the federal government sometimes finds itself at odds with state game boards, which are subject to pressures from hunters to view animals as "renewable resources" to be managed and harvested like crops. According to one survey, the number of people hunting and fishing is at an all-time high, but in some cases the seasons are being shortened or otherwise restricted.

Habitat destruction is the major force endangering animals. Critical habitat is defined as the land, water or air space used by a species for feeding, breeding, cover, shelter and normal growth and behavior. Rivers are diverted or dammed, housing is built, forests are cleared. If these activities do not actually kill the animals, they certainly make it difficult, if not impossible, for them to continue living. Sometimes efforts are made to transfer animals to another habitat or breed them in captivity, but in many countries the plight of animals is largely ignored. They are treated as a commodity, either legally or behind officials' backs.

Twenty-five to 40 percent of mammals have disappeared from North American national parks simply because there is not enough room for them. Development of areas just outside the parks' boundaries has served to push the species inward and limit their ability to roam. Apparently neither scientists nor park managers were aware of just how widespread the loss was over the last century. More species are expected to disappear in coming years.

Pollution is a problem in many places. Pesticides in particular are one of the greatest threats. The U.S. Environmental Protection Agency has planned to limit their use in areas of the country where they would affect endangered species or their habitats, but farmers have opposed this because of the cost and effectiveness of new program to eradicate pests.

Some places are distinguished by the type of and number of fauna, which make them ecologically important.

In 1938 the coelacanth, a prehistoric fish that was believed to have been extinct for 300 million years, was rediscovered in the Indian Ocean. It was fitting that the discovery was made in the waters off Madagascar, for that island republic is a virtual laboratory in the study of evolution and zoology. Once part of the African continent, it broke off about 160 million years ago, and the animal life there evolved in strange ways and retains links to its prehistoric ancestors. It is the only place where some species still exist.

The World Wildlife Fund has declared Madagascar the world's number one conservation priority because the island itself is slowly disintegrating due to erosion and deforestation, threatening the immense variety of wildlife. The people need farmland and timber; perhaps only 10 percent of the original forested land remains, and about 30 percent of that will be gone by the year 2000. Wildlife reserves have been established but they protect only one percent of the land, and the country lacks the money to enforce measures to control the destruction. The Fund, whose own resources are also limited, bears much of the burden of financing the preservation efforts. Because the land is largely unexplored, it is likely that whole species will become extinct before they are even discovered or identified.

Probably the most well-known and fascinating of Madagascar's endangered species are the aproximately 40 types of lemurs, genera *Lemur, Phaner, Hapalemur, Lepilemur, Microcebus, Allocebus, Cheirogaleus,* and *Varecia.* These intelligent arboreal primates have soft fur, long tails and snouts and large bugeyes; their ghostly appearance and nocturnal activity caused them to be named for the Latin *lemures,* the frightening spirits of the dead. Some people on Madagascar believe that the indri, *I. indri,* is their ancestor, and man does indeed share a evolutionary ancestry with this largest of lemurs.

The aye-aye, *Daubentonia madagascariensis,* like its relatives the lemurs, became scarce with the destruction of the forest because it eats insect larvae in timber, but 11 were removed to a special reserve on an offshore island. The strange animal—seemingly thrown together with, among other parts, a cat's body, a squirrel's tail, a mouse's ears, and a monkey's feet and hands—was the Fund's first project on Madagascar. It was believed by some native Malagasy peoples to be an enemy spirit and was often killed on sight, but today it seems to have been less scarce than was thought. The avahi, *Avahi laniger,* and varieties of sifaka, *Propithecus,* are other endangered types of lemurs. Among the factors that have kept their numbers low is their dislike of captivity, thereby frustrating attempts at captive breeding.

Some people on Madagascar believe that killing lemurs is taboo because of the reputed ancestral connection. Others who do not share these religious or superstitious beliefs do not hesitate to kill and eat them, because there is a shortage of protein in the human diet, meat is expensive and the animals are lucrative. Some local people, however, have been engaged in conservationist measures, such as installation of a cactus barrier around the protected habitat.

Kakadu National Park in the Northern Territory of Australia is another such place of importance. It was entered into UNESCO's World Heritage List because of the variety of animals and its 20,000-year-old rock paintings, monuments of Aboriginal culture. It is easy to understand why Aborigines consider it sacred. Kakadu is a wide canvas on which are painted mighty plains, huge escarpments, numerous waterways, great herds of water buffalo, flocks of birds, and other animals.

A wild horse gallops by 100-year-old termite mounds as big as a house. A kangaroo watches from a distance, when suddenly its joey pops its head out of its mother's pouch to inspect those who have come to inspect it. Koalas peer out from the trees; a frill-necked lizard suddenly scampers past. Alongside a billabong (pond) rests a graceful stork, ever watchful for the dreaded saltwater crocodiles lurking in the water.

The Amazon rain forest is one of the most fascinating and endangered places on Earth. Rain forests contain more than half of the world's animal species even though they cover only two percent of the Earth's surface. They provide many natural products and help stabilize the world's climate. The Amazon alone produces one-third of the world's oxygen and one-fifth of the fresh water. But those benefits are starting to disappear. A Brazilian government study has found that the river system's largest commercial fish, six to 12 feet long, have been reduced by half because of demand and overfishing, which may eventually affect the food chain. One government biologist has complained that the fishermen do not allow the fish to spawn and will use any method to kill them, including dynamite.

The region's human population has almost doubled in 15 years, and larger, more sophisticated boats are making fishing easier. Suggestions to reverse the trend include multiyear bans on fishing, restrictions on the size of catches, and mandatory fish farms to be included in hydroelectric dam projects. Many of the river's 3,000 species are also exploited by collectors, the number of aquarium fish exported tripling to 18 million between 1974 and 1985. These are not being farmed and are merely dwindling, according to one expert.

The animals are rarely seen, as though they are in hiding. They are there, but in declining numbers, as is discussed elsewhere. The forest itself is shrinking, cut down at an alarming rate to make way for development.

It is estimated that worldwide the rain forests are being cut down at the rate of 50 acres a minute. Even a short visit to these places leaves one with a profound sense of wonder, awed by the beauty and saddened by the destruction.

Now that we have an idea of the problems involved in saving animals, let us take a look at some of the species that must be saved.

MAMMALS

Primates are a large order of manmmals that includes human beings. The largest species is the gorilla, which comes in several varieties. Gorillas are almost exclusively vegetarian. Their range is from 1.5 to 11.5 square miles and they are not overly territorial. A group numbers two to 20 individuals, led by the dominant male, and the animals have social relationships. Aside from the usual amount of habitat encroachment and destruction that most endangered species face, gorillas also face the threat of poaching and injury in the traps meant for other animals. Among other measures to save gorillas, the Wildlife Preservation Trust's Jersey Zoo, in the United Kingdom's Channel Islands, maintains a breeding program for all gorillas in the British Isles.

The powerful mountain gorilla, *G. gorilla beringei*, is found in the Virunga Mountains of Rwanda, Zaire, and Uganda. It has a thick coat of long black hair. Naturalist Dian Fossey was instrumental in the fight to save this animal. She lived in Virunga National Park in Rwanda for 18 years, studying and working to protect it and its habitat from poachers, farmers and their cattle. The mountain gorilla was in danger of extinction until 1978, when a project was begun to save it in the park, which now holds about one-third of the remaining 400 gorillas. In fact, UNESCO has declared the reserve part of its Man and Biosphere Prorgram, which seeks to develop multiple uses in protected areas. It has praised the park as a standard for the management of such reserves because of the manner in which it has accommodated the needs of both the animals and the local people through development of a watershed forest. Dian Fossey was murdered by an assailant in 1985 and was buried as she wished, in a cemetery she built for the animals she loved.

Chimpanzees, *Pan troglodytes*, are among the most popular and humanlike animals. They dwell in the trees and savannahs of equatorial Africa and use tools like branches and sticks to obtain insects and vegetation for food. In an experiment testing adaptability, one researcher found the plains variety more willing than the arboreal variety to band together in defense against a predator, a dummy leopard. The savannah dwellers attacked and beat the dummy with branches, while the forest dwellers preferred flight to the safety of the trees. Even the latter variety show remarkable intelligence, building platforms in trees and manipulating their tools. But despite their intelligence, they show retrogressive tendencies in the wild and do not adapt as well as they should to the dangers facing them.

Scientists have succeeded in increasing the longevity of captive chimpanzees with veterinary medicine, but in the wild the animals face disease and acts of aggression from other animals and each other. Even in captivity the conditions they must live under are sometimes undesirable because a black market in baby chimps makes them easily obtainable, and they are considered somewhat expendable. There has been some success in returning captive or illegally obtained chimps to the wild, and the total number is believed to be about 50,000.

The pygmy chimpanzee, *Pan paniscus*, occupies a small area of rain forest in Zaire. The destruction of the high forest it lives in is the principal threat it faces. It was discovered only in the 1920s, and not much is known about it. Captive breeding programs have achieved some success, but only a few thousand remain and they are dwindling in number. The political situations in the countries these animals live in sometimes make it difficult or impracticable to study them.

The orangutan, *Pongo pygmaeus*, is another popular species because of its intelligence and appearance. Its expressive face makes it seem almost human and it is a favorite in zoos, television programs and movies. Its name means "forest man." It has extremely long, powerful arms, short legs and prehensile feet that can jut out at right angles, characteristics that make it highly adapted to life in the trees, which it rarely leaves. It is the only ape found in Asia, and the forests of Borneo and Sumatra are the only places where wild orangutans now exist. They have declined at an alarming rate in the twentieth century, especially since World War II. They are estimated to number about 2,500 or fewer. Illegal capture and export are forbidden; former attempts to capture young orangs usually entailed shooting and killing the mother, or inadvertently killing some while trapping a group. The sprawling geography of the region has aided smugglers, but the World Wildlife Fund and the IUCN have established rescue centers to repatriate captured animals to the wild.

Adding to the problem is their slow rate of reproduction and high infant mortality, especially in captivity. The animal's survival rate in captivity is not high in general. In zoos it overeats and fails to exercise, and its hair grows much longer than it would in the wild, where it would rub off on trees. It eats fruits, vegetation and small animals like frogs, birds and insects. It can usually adapt to whatever is available.

Baboons are strong and powerfully built, with jutting jaws, sharp teeth, and cheek pouches to store food. Because they live on the ground, their limbs are more equally proportioned. They are large (the body is two to four feet long, the tail another two feet) and require a large amount of food, which takes most of the day and a large area to find. Eggs and small mammals are their prey, and they in turn are the prey of big cats, snakes and eagles, but they band together to gang up on enemies. Drought, the disappearance of tall forests and the scarcity of prey threaten baboons, but they are adaptable to various conditions.

The mandrill, *Mandrillus sphinx*, of equatorial West Africa has one of the animal kingdom's most spectacular visages, scarlet, white, yellowish-orange and cobalt blue in color. Its tail region is also colorful, red, blue and violet. This fierce baboon roams forests, savannahs and rocks in large gangs. When it confronts an enemy the skin colors deepen and it assumes a threatening posture. Hunters have succeeded in diminishing the number of mandrills.

The drill, *M. leucophaeus*, has a similarly colorful rump and less colorful face. It is similar to the mandrill in its habits and habitat. The coloration, besides being a warning to enemies, is also used by the leaders of the herd to signify their dominance and as a sexual signal. The gelada baboon, *Theropithecus gelada*, a smaller species, lives in the 10,000- to 12,000-foot mountains of Ethiopia. It has a dark coat with a reddish chest, and a mane around its shoulders. Its name may have come from the Arabic word for mane. Geladas spend their days pulling up grass for food, grooming and engaging in social activities. Although they may number as many as half a million, they are threatened by farmers expanding into their hillsides and local tribes that kill large males and use their manes in ceremonies.

Gibbons, genus *Hylobates*, are small apes that swing through the forests of Southeast Asia with great speed. There are several varieties. They live in small, permanent families and are highly territorial. They are known for their haunting songs. The siamang, *Symphalangus syndactylus*, is a large black gibbon with an inflatable throat sac found in Malaysia and Indonesia.

Langurs are widely distributed though Northeast and Southeast Asia, India and Sri Lanka; in India they have survived largely because of religious taboos against killing or otherwise harming them. The entellus langur or Hanuman monkey, *Presbytis entellus*, named for the Hindu monkey god, is found around temples and is worshipped and cared for by Hindus. Normally arboreal leaf- and fruit-eaters, these langurs have adapted to the serious loss of wooded land in that overcrowded country. It is not uncommon to see them running about freely at high speed in towns and other areas occupied by humans, althought their antics— stealing food and crops—are becoming less tolerated.

Langurs live in groups of one or two dozen, sometimes more. Depending on the available area, their range may be as small as 50 acres or more than 3,000. Troupes avoid each other. Males are highly competitive and will kill each other's offspring with a savage bite to eliminate future competition and return females to the mating cycle. (Females will not mate while they are nursing, which last (12 to 20 months.) In a bizarre pattern, the bereaved mother will then mate with the killer to produce more competitive stock. Langurs have a slim chance of surviving to adulthood, although the mother will sometimes leave the group with the infants to save them.

The purple-faced langur, *P. senex*, is endangered by the loss of its habitat in Sri Lanka. In 1977 the government halted lucrative timber concessions, gem mining and treesap collecting in the Sinharaja Forest in an attempt to save it and other animals and the wet lowlands. UNESCO also contributed by declaring the area a Man and Biosphere reserve. Like the Hanuman monkey this langur is protected by religious belief, but it is also hunted for its fur and meat, and was even killed to provide food for workers during the heyday of logging operations.

Langurs in general are not often seen in zoos, because they do not fare well in captivity and are difficult to manage. Other well-known species include the Douc langur, *Pygathrix nemaeus;* Francois' langur, *Presbytis francoisi;* and the tonkin snubnosed langur, *Pygathrix* or *rhinopithecus avunculus.*

Macaques are short-tailed monkeys that live in Southeast Asia, Japan, Gibraltar and North Africa. Like langurs they have survived the shrinkage of forest land in India by supping at the table of humans or raiding their garbage. In general they are an omnivorous, highly adaptable species, eating vegetation, meat, insects and marine animals. Their social system has a highly developed hierarchy, and lesser members of the group constantly give way to the more dominant members in all matters, including quality and quantity of food. Perhaps 90 percent of the members of certain species, for instance the toque macaque, *Macaca sinica,* of Sri Lanka, die before they reach adulthood, from starvation, disease, stress and the constant fighting and harassment that are their way of life.

As though macaques do not cause each other enough suffering, they have been further subjected to human whims. In the 1950s India exporterd 200,000 a year to the West for scientific experiments, including testing of polio and other vaccines. The practice was halted in 1977, amid consternation in the scientific community, but replacements were quickly garnered from Southeast Asia, which was willing to fill the void for big money. A fraction of that number are now traded for such purposes, partly due to advances in medicine and research procedures. The Japanese macaque, *M. fuscata,* the only wild monkey in Japan, has been studied extensively and shown to have extraordinary intelligence and adaptability.

Colobus monkeys are one to two feet long, with two- to three-foot-long tails. They are found in the tropical rain forest of central Africa, swinging and running wildly through the trees in large groups. Their diet consists largely of leaves, and they must consume a great amount to be sated and properly nourished. The encroachment of humans into the forests is a major problem, as is the practice of hunting the monkeys for their fur and meat. The Tana River red colobus monkey, *Colobus badius rufomitratus,* like other red colobi, eats fresh leaves since they are higher in protein. The establishment of reserves on this Kenyan river has done much to protect this and other animals. The historic range of the Zanzibar red colubus monkey, *C.b. Kirkii,* is Tanzania, but a small colony of perhaps 200 exists on Zanzibar and is facing extinction. Attempts are being made to integrate them into populations on the mainland.

The guenon is a closely related species noted for its colorful fur and markings. Many are hunted for their pelts and flesh and because they ruin much-needed food by discarding it after a few bites. The elegant, colorful Diana monkey, *Cercopithecus diana,* with its brown, white and gray fur, moves catlike high atop the trees of coastal West Africa. L'hoest's monkey, *C. lhoesti,* has a gray beard, a dark coat and reddish markings. The red-bellied monkey, *C. erythrogaster,* inhabits western Nigeria but is extremely rare.

One of the most well-known Old World monkeys is the proboscis monkey, *Nasalis larvatus,* native to the rivers and swamps of Borneo. The male may have to move his large protuberance of a nose aside to eat, but because of its size he is also sought out by females for mating. The monkey is hunted for food by hungry natives and chased out of its habitat by developers and foresters. Reserves are slowly being established to protect it.

In the New World are found entirely different species of monkeys, including marmosets, tamarins, spider monkeys and howlers. They are endangered by the alarming rate at which humans are destroying the rain forests.

Marmosets are among the smallest monkeys, body and tail each six to 18 inches, with long, soft, beautifully colored fur and tufted hair atop their ears or gathered in a pompadour. Their furry tails sometimes have black or gray bands. They almost always remain in the trees, make loud, noisy, birdlike calls and are highly social. They eat fruits, smaller animals, insects and spiders. Not a great deal is known about them, as scientists are only beginning to study the rain forest and its wildlife.

When not endangered, marmosets have been popular as pets in Central and South America, as far back as pre-Columbian times. The conquistadors took them home to Europe and it was the fashion for women to carry them in their sleeves. Later they were discovered to be good laboratory animals, which meant large-scale exportation. The endangered species include the buff-headed marmoset, *Callithrix flaviceps*, and buffy tufted-ear marmoset, *C. jacchus aurita*, rare species of Brazil, and the cotton-top marmoset, *Saguinus oedipus*, which usually grows no bigger than a squirrel. The last species may actually be a tamarin.

Tamarins are similar to marmosets but have a different dental structure and longer limbs, which make them better jumpers. The *Leontideus* species are endangered: the golden-rumped and -headed tamarins and the golden-lion marmoset. They are so called because their shaggy manes make them look leonine. They are found in remote areas of Brazil, such areas decreasing in number due to settlements. The animals are also the object of black marketeering and there are international efforts to stop it, headed by the Jersey Wildlife Preservation Trust in the Channel Islands. The white-footed tamarin, *S.* or *Oedipomidas leucopus*, is extremely rare and inhabits riverine forests in central Colombia.

Howler monkeys are aptly named, for they make incredibly loud sounds. Early in the morning in the jungle, distant groups announce their territory by howling. Rival groups that encounter each other determine superiority by which howls the loudest. They also warn enemies or call for help in this way. They can be ferocious and difficult to tame. Depending on a group's population and the amount of food available, they may adapt to less than virgin forests or separate into exclusive territories. They are not especially intelligent and do not engage in mutual grooming, which allows parasites to lay eggs in their fur. They are also susceptible to recurring epidemics of yellow fever. They move slowly and are easily taken by hunters. The black howler monkey, *Alouatta pigra*, is threatened throughout its range in Mexico, Guatemala and Belize.

Spider monkeys, *Ateles geoffroyi*, are among the larger New World species. Even among species as agile in general as monkeys, these are known as acrobats. They use their long, prehensile tails to swing through the trees of Central America in groups. With them they grasp branches and keep their hands free to grasp other objects, which they may hurl down at enemies. They can leap 30 feet in one bound. They eat jungle vegetation and fruit and chatter loudly to scare away enemies when necessary. Like many animals, the spider monkey has not always fared well in captivity, and efforts to induce captive breeding have been futile. The woolly spider monkey, *Brachyteles arachnoides*, has been endangered by the cultivation of the forests of southern Brazil between the Parana River and the coast. It is rare; about 300 remain.

Sakis and uakaris are closely related. The rare white-nosed saki, *Chiropotes albinasus*, of southern Brazil numbers only about four and is in great danger of extinction. Uakaris (genus *Cacajao*) are bald monkeys that live in Peru, Brazil, Ecuador, Colombia and Venezuela. The three species do not overlap one another's range. The red-faced uakari lives in the forests of the Amazon Basin. Its face is a truly strange contrast to its fur.

Almost every child in the West at some point owns a teddy bear, the very symbol of childhood. This adorable quality makes bears high-profile glamour animals on the endangered list, but they too are misunderstood. They are responsible for increased public consciousness about the environment and conservation, but the increased tourism in their habitats sometimes taxes the land. Bears seldom leave their habitat and confront humans; when they do they often eat vegetables or kill farm animals, which makes them unwelcome. They are mostly vegetarian, except in the spring, when they emerge from hibernation and little food is available. They eat berries and salmon but will also eat moose in a pinch. They have been the stuff of legend (Goldilocks) and cruel sport (bear-baiting) and the victim of trophy hunters and gourmet cooks (bear paw being one delicacy served in China).

The brown bear, *Ursus a. arctos*, which is common throughout the Northern Hemisphere, was the subject of a study in Italy, one of the places where it faces special danger. Mountain farmers in the Abruzzi area had taken to killing them because of their frequent raids on livestock and crops. The World Wildlife Fund compensated the farmers for whatever was lost, determined the boundaries of the feeding area, and expanded the national park to include it. Sixty to 100 bears remain. Similar action was taken in the alpine Trentino Valley, where only a handful survive, and a guard was posted to monitor poaching.

In the United States the brown bear or grizzly, *U.a. horribilis*, has threatened status. It can grow to 7.5 feet long and 800 pounds. Hardly any other animal is a match for its incredible strength; it can break a bison's neck with one blow. Smaller grizzlies are sometimes mistaken for black bears and killed by hunters. The grizzly does not reproduce well and its numbers are difficult to estimate, much less determine accurately, but there may be only about 200, few of them female, in the 5.5 million acres of Yellowstone National Park. It is believed that fewer than half of all cubs reach maturity. The Mexican variety, *U. a. nelsoni*, may have been exterminated by the poisons set out by cattlemen angered by the bears' raids on their ranches. The Asian variety, *U. a. pruinosus*, and especially the Baluchistan bear, *U. thibetanus gedrosianus*, have also been greatly hunted.

The giant panda, *Ailuropoda melanoleuca*, shares a common ancestry with both bears and raccoons, but some scientists say it occupies a niche all its own. It was adopted as the symbol of the World Wildlife Fund because it is cute, cuddly and one of the rapidly shrinking species on the endangered list. It is currently engaged in a life-and-death struggle in its native China, as conservationists and the Chinese government try to protect it in specially created reserves and "pandaminiums." Two major factors in its decline are the periodic flowering of bamboo, whose scarcity robs it of its main food source, and its difficulty in reproducing. Captive breeding programs have been tried in zoos around the world, but few have been successful. In 1976 145 pandas lived in the Wolong Reserve in Sichuan province, studied and cared for by scientists, but the number was halved by early 1988.

Poaching has traditionally been a severe problem. Pandas are sometimes ensnared in traps set for other animals, such as the Asian musk deer, but they are also slain for their pelts, which are smuggled to Japan and Hong Kong for top dollar. Conservationists thought they had the problem licked through publicity about the animals' plight and the posting of rewards for peasants who rescue starving pandas, but in early 1988 the Chinese government arrested 203 people, and was seeking 150 more, for poaching 146 pandas. The number was thought to represent one-seventh of all remaining pandas, a serious setback to the efforts to keep them alive. Twenty-six of the poachers were found guilty and sentenced to prison terms of one year to life; others faced penalties as severe as death.

Folklore has done much to fan the flames of primal fear about wolves, which have traditionally suffered both image problems and hysterical persecution. Wolves are nocturnal hunters, often traveling 40 to 50 miles a night in pursuit of quarry. They have a highly developed social system and usually mate for life. They have been hunted and killed in great numbers by humans, sometimes federal trappers in predator-control programs, protecting livestock and game. One way of keeping the wolf from taking such animals has been to ensure the supply of its prey species, such as nutria, which resembles a muskrat.

The red wolf, *Canis rufus*, a rare animal, is endangered over its range in the southern United States from Florida to Texas, and is extinct in the wild. About 80 remain in captivity. An experimental population has been established in several counties of North Carolina to try and recover it. Identification of true red wolves has been difficult because of their hybridization with coyotes; it may indeed become extinct simply though extended breeding with other canids until it completely dilutes its line. The gray wolf, *C. lupus*, has also been the victim of bad publicity, but it helps keep down the population of such animals as moose, which can ruin a forest though overgrazing. It is endangered in the lower 48 states except for Minnesota, where it is threatened.

The maned wolf, *Chrysocyon brachyurus*, ranges over South America between southern Brazil and northern Argentina. Like others of its kind it has been unjustly accused of killing domestic animals, which it only occasionally does, and has suffered the vengeance of farmers as a result. Actually, it mostly eats small mammals and birds in the wild. The World Wildlife Fund has helped capture maned wolves to fit them with radio collars for study in Brazil's Serra da Canastra National Park.

Foxes have suffered the same bad image as wolves, even though they benefit farmers by keeping down the number of rodents. There are several kit foxes, but the San Joaquin variety, *Vulpes macrotis mutica*, found in

California, faces the greatest danger. It has adapted well to its desert environment through its small size and large ears, which release body heat. The swift fox inhabits Canada and the northern plains of the United States. It eats mice, small mammals, insects and fruit. The northern variety, *V. velox hebes*, is endangered in Canada. Neither the kit fox nor the swift fox is very wary and both face danger from trappers.

The hyena lies somewhere biologically between the wild dogs and the big cats. It is a scavenger that roams at night, but it is also a predator. It is distinguished by its cry, which sounds like strange laughter. Hyenas use their strong jaws to crush bones. They feed on carrion littering the plains of Africa and Asia and hunt down packs of animals like zebras. The carnivorous hyena has coarse hair and short back legs. It has earned its place in legend and literature, partly because of its "laughter." Even though the brown hyena, *Hyaena brunnea*, is protected, farmers kill it in southern Africa because it attacks livestock. The Barbary hyena, *H. h. barbara*, inhibits Morocco, Algeria and Tunisia.

The legendary and popular lion occupies a special place in folklore. It is found mainly in the savannahs of sub-Saharan Africa. Kenya has estimated that a single live lion is worth more than $500,000 in tourist revenues, whereas a dead one brings only about $8,500 and its skin only about $1,000. Kenya and other African countries have therefore done a great deal to protect and preserve it. Its Asiatic or Indian cousin has not fared so well, having virtually disappeared. A few remain in India, but they ranged historically as far afield as Turkey, Iran and Arabia.

The Asiatic lion, *Panthera leo persica*, is similar to the African variety but has a heavier coat and a smaller mane. As with so many other animals, hunting was the bane of its existence until it was officially protected and the last area it inhabited, the Gir Forest of northwestern India, was established as a wildlife sanctuary. But the lions shared this land with farmers, whose domestic animals were eating the vegetation and natural cover. The farmers were also burning much of the cover, and few of the wild animals the lions hunted were available. The lions turned to the domestic animals for food, and the angered farmers in turn poisoned the lions. The solution was to declare the area a national park and move the farmers and their animals to other areas, allowing the forest to regenerate and the natural game to return. Captive breeding was also introduced.

The lion is traditionally thought of as the king of beasts, but some would argue that it is at best a pretender to the throne of the tiger, *Panthera tigris*, one of the noblest animals in nature and one of the most threatened. Found throughout Asia's forests, this beautiful creature has long been hunted for its distinctive pelt, yellow-orange with black stripes. Despite its size and strength (males reach 10 feet in length and weigh up to 650 pounds) it is no match for a cunning hunter or the more subtle forms of destruction it faces.

India is a principal part of the animal's range, and it was there that the major focus of the campaign to save it has taken place. In 1930, during British rule, there were 40,000 tigers in India alone, and they were hunted freely by maharajas and white hunters. Because firearms were widely available after independence was granted in 1947, poachers proliferated. Modern development, trying to keep pace with the needs of the growing human population, threatened the tiger's habitat. Even today villagers start forest fires to improve the quality of grass for cattle, but this destroys the undergrowth, sometimes killing tiger cubs, birds, and other animals and upsetting the balance of nature. Cubs also face danger from leopards, hyenas, wild dogs and snakes, and rarely does more than one cub from a litter survive its first year.

By 1970 the number of tigers had dropped to 5,000 in all of Asia. Other species of tiger had died out or faced imminent extinction, so in 1972 the World Wildlife Fund began Project Tiger, whose goal was to recover the Indo-Chinese variety. In the process, India's forests, so vital to the ecological balance, would also benefit through restoration. The project was designed to monitor poaching and guard against the danger of fire, using vehicles, elephant transportation, communication equipment and modern technology. The Indian government contributed $5 million and the Fund raised another $1 million.

Through the efforts of the IUCN, the government banned tiger hunting. Prime Minister Indira Gandhi, a Project Tiger committee chairwoman, established a task force to study the animal's needs. Almost 90 percent of the country's forests had disappeared, and humans inhabited the rest. Eleven tiger reserves were established throughout the country with funds raised from an international appeal. Thirty-three villages were relocated to make way for the reserves, partly through Mrs. Gandhi's efforts. Villagers were given new lands, timber and funds to build houses in a program that is continuing. The government now spends about $30 million a year on Project Tiger and the reserves.

In 10 years the number of tigers was more than doubled, but problems remain in establishing enough territory to support the growing population. About 1,800 of India's approximately 4,000 tigers live in reserves, but the rest live wherever they can find food, water and forested or long-grass regions. They have adapted to diverse ecological conditions and exist in near-deserts and salty mangrove forests. Worldwide the population now stands at about 9,000, including about 1,500 in zoos. The environmental protection campaign on the reserves has increased not only the tiger population, but also that of other wildlife and endangered species such as the swamp deer, the Asian elephant and the rhinoceros. The land, vegetation and systems of waterways have also benefited, as have the people, another part of the ecosystem. Some who were formerly hunters have been retrained as game wardens as part of the conservation program.

The cheetah, *Acinonyx jubatus*, outruns its prey with sheer blinding speed. It is the fastest four-footed animal, exceeding 60 mph in short bursts. This spotted cat uses its long tail for balance and keeps its head motionless while chasing prey to keep it in sight. It has survived since the days of the ancient Egyptians, who kept it as a pet. Later, Arabs and Indians actually used it as a hunting animal.

The cheetah was once found throughout Africa and central Asia, but today only a few scattered populations exist outside Africa. Hunted for its pelt, it has already become extinct in most of its former range. Its African habitat meanwhile is increasingly being transformed into cropland to feed the human population of a largely starving continent, and the animals it stalks, like antelope and gazelle, are declining. Although it breeds plentifully, seven out of 10 cubs die before maturity, the victims of disease, malnutrition, bigger cats and hyenas, and the life span is only four to five years. About 1,000 cheetahs exist in the vicinity of Serengeti National Park in Tanzania, and maintaining the vast amount of land they need is the key to saving them.

The leopard, *P. pardus*, is endangered in most of its range of Asia and Africa and only threatened in the African nations of Gabon, Congo, Zaire, Uganda and Kenya. Small numbers are found ranging from Israel, where it was thought to have been extinct, to the Korean Peninsula. The Israeli government's establishment of wildlife reserves brought back the ibex and other animals, which in turn brought back the leopard as a predator. It is quiet and solitary, hunting mostly at night, especially when it knows that poachers are about. Their hunt for its valuable pelt and the destruction of the cover it needs to stalk prey are its nemeses. It is also disliked and hunted by farmers because it kills their livestock. Despite this it has shown a remarkable ability to survive under a variety of conditions, including deserts, jungles and snowy mountains. The leopard's whiskers function as antennae as it hunts. It eats monkeys, antelopes, jackals, peacocks and large porcupines, and has even been known to attack humans. It will eat fish and smaller game if necessary, and it thinks nothing of tackling far bigger prey, being strong enough to carry its kill up into a tree to eat it.

The snow leopard or ounce, *P. uncia*, with its thick, insulating fur, is specifically adapted to the coldness of the Himalayas and other Asian mountain ranges. Unlike its relative it has been unable to adapt to life anywhere else and is extremely rare. The hair on the soles of its feet protects them and gives it traction in its habitat, at 10,000 to 20,000 feet. Humans are increasingly invading this territory and meeting the snow leopard when it descends in winter. Like other big cats it must turn to livestock when its wild prey, like sheep, and vegetation are scarce, and it is then killed in retaliation. The world's fashion industry also seeks its warm, grayish-white spotted coat. There are only about 1,000 of these cats left, including a few hundred in captive breeding programs. If scientists are able to breed them in zoos and reintroduce them into the wild, they will still face the problem of a shrinking habitat.

In the forests of the New World, the jaguar, *P. onca*, is king, but one that is being pushed further into exile. Once common in the southeastern United States, today the Western Hemisphere's largest cat is rarely seen north of the Mexican border. Whether it inhabits the pampas, the brushlands, the mountains or the rain forest, it always stays near water, which it will even enter to attack a caiman. Like its relatives, it often kills cattle, for which jungles have been cleared for grazing land, and suffers the vengeance of the farmers. The trade in pelts, which hurt the animal's numbers, has been banned. Just how many jaguars remain no one knows.

Another lordly cat is *Felis concolor*, which goes by scores of names, including mountain lion, puma, cougar, panther and many colorful colloquial ones. Although the various species are endangered they have survived even modern urbanization. They are found in virtually every environment in the Western Hemisphere. Since whitetail deer have surged in population in eastern North America, the eastern cougar, *F.c. cougar*, has not lacked for this staple of its diet and has also expanded its numbers. But its abilities as a hunter have made it a pest, and it has then been hunted nearly to extinction itself. Other endangered varieties include the Florida panther, *F.c. coryi*, and the Costa Rican puma, *F.c. costaricensis*.

Some scientists believe that the clouded lepard, *Neofelis nebulosa*, found hanging by its paws in southeastern and south-central Asia and Taiwan, is an evolutionary link between larger and smaller cats. Smaller than a true leopard, it is nevertheless deadly. Its fangs are larger than any other cat's, and its raspy tongue helps it lick the meat from the bones of its kill. It has been hunted for its yellow-brown, black-banded coat, but either its declining numbers or the effectiveness of measures prohibiting trade in it have made the fur scarce.

Many smaller cats are grouped under the genus *Felis*. These include several species of jaguarundi, *F. yagouaroundi*, located in Central America. Jaguarundis resemble weasels and have been useful in hunting rats. The margay, *F. wiedii*, and ocelot, *F. pardalis*, also mainly Central and South American, have been part of the lucrative fur trade, as has been their Iberian counterpart, the Spanish lynx, *F. lynx pardina*, with its startling appearance and beautiful coat. The leopard cat, *F. b. bengalensis*, needs a huge amount of territory in Indian and Southeast Asian forests in which to roam, and the destruction of that habitat and its prey by pesticides endangers it. Meanwhile the bobcat, *F. rufus*, has shifted its habitat from its former range in central Mexico and now is scattered throughout the United States and southern Canada.

In North America deer are fairly hardy and common, the victims of annual, state-sanctioned hunts and frequent, fatal collisions with automobiles. There are, however, endangered species. Besides predators like mountain lions, bears and wolves, the Columbian white-tailed deer, *Odocoileus virginianus leucurus*, has faced human encroachment and overhunting in its traditional range in Washington and Oregon. Likewise, the key deer, *O.v. clavium*, has declined with the large-scale development of the Florida Keys, and has disappeared from many. A pale deer with small antlers, it would swim from one island to another, but has been eliminated from several by human encroachment, wild, unrestrained hunting parties and natural disasters like hurricanes. The designation of a national wildlife refuge and stiff enforcement of the rules regarding protection have allowed the species to recover. The Cedros Island mule deer, *O. hemionus cedrosensis*, faces similar problems in its Mexican habitat. In the mid-1970s four South American deer were identified as being at special risk and were the subject of a special study for management and recovery. They were the marsh deer, *Blastocerus dichotomus;* the pampas deer, *Ozotoceros bezoarticus;* and two varieties of huemuls—the North Andean, *Hippocamelus antisensis*, and South Andean, *H. bisulcus*. The endangered status of the the latter two animals in Chile, which are among the smallest deer, had already been noted in studies aided by the U.S. Peace Corps, among other groups, and a more exhaustive study was undertaken to study the effects of development in the cold rain forest.

The sika is considered one of the most attractive members of the deer family, but it has also been one of the least protected. The Formosan sika deer, *C. nippon taiouanus*, has vanished from the wild but survives in zoos. It was declared extinct in its native habitat of Taiwan in 1973 because of poaching by the aboriginal peoples of the central highlands. On Taiwan as in other places in the Orient there exists a large industry built around herbal and other non-traditional medicines, and the deer's antlers are believed to have healing powers. The North China sika deer, *C.n. mandarinus*, found in Shandong province in the People's Republic of China, was once common in northeastern China and was protected by the various dynastic rulers, but Manchu soldiers routinely slaughtered it in the Imperial Hunting Grounds in what is now Chengde. After the overthrow of the Manchu, the final dynasty, the deer declined. The Shanxi sika, *C.n. grassianus*, of Shanxi province, was hunted in August and September, when its antlers were at their height. The antlers would be cut off, shorn of their velvet, dried, shredded and boiled in soup. The South China sika, *C.n. kopschi*, found throughout the south, faces similar dangers because of its reputed aphrodisiac powers.

Woodland caribou, *Rangifer tarandus caribou*, also known as wild reindeer, are large animals reaching eight feet in length, four feet at shoulder height, and 600 pounds. They are unique in the deer family in that both the male and the female have antlers. They are endangered in parts of southern Canada, Idaho and Washington and are far scarcer there than in northern Europe and Asia. As with other animals, logging activities pose the principal threat, although poaching is also a problem. Caribou migrate south to the forest in the winter and return north to the tundra in the spring. Activities such as the construction of pipelines interrupt their route. The elevated Trans-Alaska Pipeline was especially disruptive. Nursing females in particular feared for their young, while adult males did not seem to be affected, and this was thought to be a potential threat to the unity of the herds. Studies are still underway to determine the long-range effects.

Pronghorns are antelope-like ruminants found in the prairies and deserts of western North America. They are fast runners and good swimmers, and warn one another of danger with their erect tail hairs. Both the peninsular pronghorn, *Antilocapra americana peninsularis*, of Baja California, and the Sonoran pronghorn, *Antilocapra americana sonoriensis*, found elsewhere in Mexico and in Arizona, face threats from hunting, habitat disappearance and competitiion for grazing land from livestock. There is scientific debate over whether they should occupy their own family, because of the hairlike antler sheaths that are shed annually, or be classified as part of the Bovid family.

Bovids make up a large family of herbivorous ungulates containing such members as antelopes, sheep and buffalo. Despite the horns of many species, they are mostly unable to defend themselves against predators. This and the destruction of their habitat place them in great danger of extinction.

The Western giant eland, *Taurotragus d. derbianus*, is the largest antelope, reaching as much as 11.5 feet in length and weighing a ton. It has long, spiralling horns and vertical stripes down its sides. It is found in Senegal, Mali and Guinea but has become extinct in the Ivory Coast. Laws have failed to protect it from tribesmen, who hunt it for its meat and leathery hide; disease also takes its toll.

Impalas can leap 10 feet into the air and 30 feet in one bound. They are non-territorial under certain conditions and live in herds of up to 60 animals. Males of species such as the black-faced impala, *Aepyceros melampus peteirs*, will normally stake out territory for mating and fight off bachelor intruders. But with the onset of drought, the territories and hierarchies fall apart and each animal fends for itself in the struggle to survive and find food.

Several varieties of gazelle inhabit much of Africa, and they are among the more endangered animals. They are two-toned as protective coloration against predators. They have been fairly abundant in some countries while in others they have been hunted to near extinciton. Because soldiers and government workers have often used automatic weapons on them for target practice, hunting has been curtailed. But tribesmen also hunt them, finding them more able than cattle to survive desert conditions and provide food. The Arabian oryx, *Oryx leucoryx*, was, ironically, saved from extinction by domestication, although it has disappeared in the wild.

The slender-horned gazelle, *Gazella leptoceros*, or rhim, is abut 2.5 feet at the shoulder and weighs about 60 pounds. It is found in the northern Sahara from Algeria to Egypt and Sudan. It can survive under harsh conditions in the desert, although it will leave to find food during drought. In former times the desert habitat was often fatal to this gazelle because the footsteps of stalkers could not be heard. While the advent of motor vehicles increased the mobility of hunters in general, they could not negotiate the desert, so it fared better, unlike the Arabian gazelle, *G.g. arabica*, and Saudi Arabian gazaelle, *G. dorcas saudiya*, both scattered throughout the Middle East. The environment also hindered study of the animals and protective measures. This is unfortunate because study of their adaptability could benefit other forms of life.

The Arabian oryx became extinct in the wild in the 1970s but it was reintroduced into a region of Oman by a local people. It prefers gravel plains but will move to the desert when threatened or to find vegetation during heavy rains. It was formerly hunted on camels but motor vehicles made the hunt easier, if not more sporting. The oryx is prized as a delicacy, for its hide, and even for medicinal purposes such as snakebite cure. The Sultan of Oman took a personal interest in the animal in the 1960s, ordering local Bedouins to refrain from hunting it. This, however, did not prevent others not under the Sultan's domain from continuing. Leaders of some Arab nations in the modern era have embarked upon extravagant, self-indulgent hunts reminiscent of ancient times, but other nations have established captive breeding programs and reserves to help it.

The walia or Abyssinian ibex, *Capra walie*, lives between 8.000 and 11,00 feet in the mountains of Ethiopia, feeding on vegetation. It easily negotiates the mountainous country, which thwarts some hunters. Yet it is still hunted and its horns are used as drinking goblets. It is said that the Italian occupation before World War II, during which guerrillas took to the mountains, began the onslaught against the ibex, for the hungry guerrillas slaughtered it for food. After the war firearms proliferated and it was hunted on a large scale. The Spanish variety, the Pyrenean ibex, *C.p. pyrenaica*, is also endangered.

The hartebeest, a relative of the gnu with lyre-shaped horns. is also similiar to the horse in physiology and swiftness. Two varieties of hartebeest are on the endangered list: Swayne's hartebeest, *Alcelaphus buselaphus swaynei*, found in Ethiopia but eliminated from Somalia, and the tora hartebeest, *A.b. tora*, of Ethiopia, Sudan and Egypt. A hundred years ago the plains contained thousands of these antelopes, but rinderpest, a contagious cattle virus that ulcerates the intestines, decimated the herds. Military campaigns at the turn of the century also allowed professional hunters and amateurs among the soldiers unlimited access. Although the animals' numbers are small, the problem of widespread famine seems to be at odds with the concept of conservation.

The wild yak, *B. grunniens*, once common in Tibet and India, is now rare, but has been bred into a smaller, more manageable beast of burden by the farmers of that rugged region. Both species are surefooted, able climbers and function well at altitudes upward of 17,000 feet. They subsist on what little vegetation is available and keep warm with their shaggy coats, which provide wool for humans as well. The few yaks that have not been hunted to extinction are used to plow the land and pull heavy loads. They are also used for their milk, meat and leather.

Wild goats live in herds. They are also bred for their milk and wool, which provides cashmere and mohair. Several species of wild goat face danger. The Kabal markhor, *Capra falconeri megaceros*, and straight-horned markhor, *C.f. jerdoni*, would be difficult to study in their habitat in the rugged mountains of Pakistan and Afghanistan under ordinary conditions, but the situation has been compounded by the long, bloody war and the stream of refugees there. Few researchers are willing to study animals under such conditions, nor should they be expected to. The animals, however, suffer because of this. The name markhor means "snake-eater"; the animal is believed to eat snakes, and its meat is used as an antitoxin for snakebite. The Apennine chamois, *R. rupicapra ornata*, is an Italian variety of the nimble mountain goat that makes tremendous leaps through the spectacular mountains of Europe and the Middle East. It can survive hostile weather and up to two weeks without food.

Two animals in particular symbolize the plight of wildlife. The first is the wood bison, *B. bison athabascae*, often incorrectly called a buffalo. It has long roamed North America and is especially endangered in Canada. At one time there were 60 million wood bison in the American West. The number dwindled to a few hundred a century ago because of large-scale slaughter that began with European settlers, but they have made a slow recovery to several thousand. Programs have concentrated on eliminating individuals with diseases such as tuberculosis and anthrax, since such illnesses spread quickly, and on captive breeding to maintain this symbol of the heritage of a continent.

The second animal is the argali, *O. ammon hodgsoni*, a large sheep with huge horns that can reach six feet in length. It inhabits the top of the world, the Himalayas, a habitat that until relatively recently was unspoiled and unvisited. As humans increasingly overrun this great sanctuary, the animals climb higher and retreat deeper into its recesses, a proud metaphor for the spirit of nature in one of Earth's holiest places.

The elephant is a beautiful. intelligent animal, the largest on land. It too symbolizes the struggles of all wild animals. An elephant gestates for about two years. The young will live with the mother as part of the matriarchal herd for another eight to 12 years, and these highly societal animals develop complex relationships. The trunk is a combination nose and upper lip. It is powerful enough to lift tree trunks yet sensitive enought to grasp a single fruit. No mammal has anything like it; only the tentacles of an octopus are at all similar. The elephant plays an important role as a domestic animal in such industries as logging, and it has often been exploited in such other operations as the transportation of heavy equipment for armies.

The Asian elephant, *Elephas maximus*, found from India to Indonesia, has smaller ears and tusks than the African elephant, *Loxodonta africana*, found mostly in the central part of the continent. There are large numbers of elephants remaining, an estimated 30,000 to 40,000 Asian and perhaps 1.3 million African, but they are considered endangered because of the constant threat of poaching and the human pressure exerted on their habitat. They have become extinct in several countries.

The hunting of elephants for their ivory tusks has greatly reduced their numbers. Japan and Hong Kong are the biggest importers of African ivory, accounting for 80 percent of the world total in some years. Even when some countries have banned raw-ivory exports, the purchasers have simply gone elsewhere. The tusks are used as elaborate conversation pieces and intricately carved ornaments. The establishment of reserves in Africa did so much to protect elephants that they were threatened by their own burgeoning numbers, for they reproduce quickly in adequate living conditions. But they are destructive to the environment and dangerous to each other when their habitat becomes overcrowded and grasslands are scarce. Poachers have often taken advantage of such situations, feeling that the elephants were doomed anyway. The price of ivory increased tenfold between 1969 and 1979, and 50,000 to 100,000 elephants per year were slaughtered. The political situation in some countries has allowed such practices to flourish. Because of the thickness of their skin, elephants were once scientifically classified with hippopotamuses, rhinoceroses and tapirs, but they are not related.

Its tanklike appearance and dangerous-looking horn make the rhinoceros feared and misunderstood. It is actually responsible for fewer attacks on humans than is believed, the hippo, for instance, being more deadly than it looks. Rhinos are slaughtered for their horns, which are made into dagger handles and are reputed to have medicinal and aphrodisiac powers. These products are especially valued in the Middle East and the Far East. A rhino-horn ceremonial dagger, popular as a status symbol with the oil-rich in North Yemen, can cost as much as U.S. $1,000. As a result the animals face great danger from poachers and must be strictly protected. Their numbers have shrunk from 45,000 in 1970 to about 6,000.

The black rhino, *Diceros bicornis*, inhabits sub-Saharan Africa and is particularly endangered in Zimbabwe, its numbers there down to about 2,000. An anti-poaching patrol has been established in the Zambezi Valley, and other conservation plans are in the works. In general the black rhino declined from about 15,000 in 1980 to fewer than 9,000 in 1984. The white rhino's name may merely be a corruption of the Dutch word for wide; the rhino is usually gray or brown. An adult male stands six-and-a-half feet at the shoulder and weighs three tons. The northern white rhino, *Ceratotherium simum cottoni*, traditionally inhabited several countries in central Africa, but it faces imminent extinction, the total population having declined to about 20. The southern variety has benefited from conservation programs; it may have been exterminated in certain areas and then reintroduced from others. The animals sometimes are partially recovered through the efforts of conservation organizations, only to suffer again with the outbreak of wars or civil unrest.

The great Indian rhino, *Rhinoceros unicornis*, has special cultural significance in Nepal and almost every part is used. The government has taken steps to protect it in national parks such as Citawan, and poaching has been controlled. The Javan rhino, *R. sondaicus*, formerly found throughout Asia from India to Indonesia, now numbers only about 50, although the number is increasing. The Sumatran rhino, *Didermoceros sumatrensis*, besides being the smallest (five feet at the shoulder, weighing a half-ton), has the added disadvantage of an extra horn.

The tapir is related to the rhinoceros and the horse. All four varieties are endangered by the destruction of the forest, encroachment by man, and the introduction of domestic animals into the habitat. The tapir spends much of its time in the water and mud of the rain forest and in mountains. It has been found in lowlands swamps and 10,000-foot mountains. Despite its round, stubby, somewhat awkward appearance it is a good swimmer, fast runner and expert climber. The Central American tapir, *Tapirus bairdii*, stands about 3.5 feet at the shoulder. Not much is know about it, but zoos like the Emilio Goeldi Museum in Belem, Brazil, study the Brazialian variety, *T. terrestris*, and display it in its natural habitat. The mountain tapir, *T. pinchaque*, is striped when young but loses the stripes in adulthood. The Asian tapir, *T. indicus*, is the only variety found outside Central and South America.

Few wild horses exist today. Przewalski's horse, *Equus przewalskii*, is believed to have been the ancestor of all domestic varieties. The harsh, forbidding country of its habitat in northern China has helped isolate it from human encroachment, but it has faced competition and dilution of its basic stock from domestic varieties. It is difficult to identify the horse and follow its movements, if indeed it still exists in the wild, because it can be easily mistaken for a similar species, the Mongolian wild ass. It has been bred successfully in captivity.

Zebras are among the most recognizable of animals, except to predators, which are confused by their stripes in the tall grasses of Africa. They normally travel great distances every day to find waterholes in their semi-desert surroundings. There are differences between zebras, notably in the arrangement or length of stripes. Grevy's zebra, *E. grevyi*, has symmetrical stripes that end near its belly, which is white. The only remaining mountain zebras, *E.z. zebra*, live in reserves in South Africa, but even there they face danger from hunters, as well as drought and diseases like anthrax. They were protected as early as 1656, but hunting laws were later relaxed and the animals were killed in large numbers. They have recovered in recent years, numbering more than 100. Hartmann's mountain zebra, *E.z. hartmannae*, numbers several thousand in Namibia but has been declining. One reaseon is that fences ostensibly erected for the animals' own good instead restricted their seasonal movements, preventing them from reaching water.

Of the two species of camel, the Bactrian camel, *Camelus bactrianus*, is endangered. It is a staple of transportation and commerce in areas such as northern China, where it has performed its function for centruries. The shaggy, two-humped camel was part of the ancient Silk Road, on which trade flourished for a thousand years. Few of these animals are wild, their stock having been diluted with domestic. They have been hunted for their meat and skin, a practice now outlawed; today one may see them in zoos or giving the Chinese equivalent of a pony ride to tourists at the Great Wall. The camel sheds its hair in summer. It is a distant relative of the vicuña.

The vicuña, *V. icugna*, found in the Andes, is valued for its soft, warm fleece. The ancient Incas sheared the animals annually, but the Spanish conquistadors merely killed and skinned them. A vicuña reserve in Peru has recovered the animals, bringing the number from 1,500 in 1967 to 48,000 in 1980, 80 percent of the world population. But the program was so successful that they may have been prematurely culled. The Peruvian government's ban on the export of vicuña wool and the end of imports by other countries have helped save the animal.

Prairie dogs, *Cynomys parvidens*, live in "towns," some of which have been know to extend for 100 miles and include millions of the highly social animals. The prairie dog feeds in 30- to 40-seconds bursts, then stops to check its surroundings carefully for any sign of danger. It is a nuisance to farmers and ranchers because it eats grass. The elimination of bison and other large animals helped the prairie dog to flourish because it reduced the competition for grazing land. In recent years the development of land has diminished its habitat, and a large-scale campaign to eliminate it through poisoning and destruction of its burrows also threatens other animals that do no damage.

The black-footed ferret, *Mustela nigripes*, a 1.5-foot-long, weasel-like animal once prominent in western North America, today has virtually vanished and may be America's rarest mammal. Only one colony of 31 remains, in Wyoming, although it has tripled in number in just a few years. The mass extermination campaign against the prairie dog also affected the ferret, which depends on it as food and for its burrows.

The Mongolian variety of beaver, *Castor fiber birulai*, is a highly societal rodent. The dams built by beaver communities create necessary ponds and pastures, and the animals' threatened extinction also threatens these areas. The Vancouver Islan marmot, *Marmota vancouverensis*, hunted for its soft, warm far, is a fairly sociable animal that lives in a den. After eating, it perches on high ground to whistle a warning of intruders. Wolves, eagles and bears are among its enemies. Its vision and hearing are keen, and it makes several sounds to express its emotional state. Marmots hibernate in the winter and mate as soon as they come out. Some remain near the den year-round; others travel far afield.

The small, mouselike chinchilla, *Chinchilla brevicaudata boliviana*, was once common in theAndes but was exhaustively hunted for its thick coat, which brings great prices on world fur markets.

Mice and rats are among the most disliked of animals, and it is difficult for most people to muster any sympathy for them. They carry disease, eat grain, fruits and nuts, and are a general nuisance, but they also eat many insects. Many of these animals are endangered because of the intense efforts to exterminate them and because of predators like owls and larger mammals. Many species are rare or not easily studied, and therefore there is not a great deal of information about them. Among the endangered species are kangaroo rats, genus *Dipodomys*, small, leaping rodents that live in the deserts of North America. They are also called pocket rats because they carry food in their cheek pouches.

Marsupials come in all shapes and sizes, but most have an external pouch in which the female carries its young. Some resemble mice; an Australian species is in fact called marsupial-mouse, genus *Sminthopsis*. Others are larger, like wallabies and kangaroos. The male red kangaroo, *Macropus rufus*, may reach more than seven feet in height and weigh more than 200 pounds.

Kangaroos have been both a symbol of Australia and a subject of great controversy there and in conservation circles. Hunters are allowed to take a certain number every year; about 2.5 million are killed legally. Some experts say this will lead to the extinciton of the red and the gray kangaroos; others say they have an unlimited capacity for reproduction. A 1982 drought reduced their number from 19 million to 10 million, but within four years they had increased to 16 million. The often cruel methods that amateur "sport" hunters use to torture and unnecessarily kill them are the target of conservation efforts and international outrage. One suggested solution is the use of kangaroos for meat, since they are well-suited to the arid climate and provide more meat than other animals while eating the same amount of grass.

Some species of rat-kangaroo, genus *Bettongia*, do not fear humans and thus suffer greatly at their hands. They will playfully enter camps, only to be attacked by dogs and red foxes. The wallaby is a smaller relative of the kangaroo. Both animals raise young in the same manner and can hop at about 30 mph. The bridled nail-tailed wallaby, *Onychogqalea fraenata*, and crescent nail-tailed wallaby, *O. lunata*, each have a fingernail-like scale at the end of the tail, hence the name. The former variety is endangered by hunters, predators like foxes and competition for food from rabbits. The quokka, *Setonix brachyurus*, which more resembles a large rat than a kangaroo, also must contend with hunters as it scavenges and tries to find water in the area near Perth.

Leaving the continent down under we journey to the New World to find the giant armadillo, *Priodontes maximus*, and the pink fairy armadillo, *Chlamyphorus truncatus*. The giant armadillo, 3.5 feet long with a 20-inch tail, is covered with armorlike scales. It stands on its hind legs and tail while it rips apart a termite mound with its long claws. It feeds on all manner of insects, worms, snakes and spiders. The pink fairy, six inches long and bearing pale pink armor, feeds on ants, worms, snails and plants. It has not fared well in captivity. With their short, stubby legs, armadillos are not champion runners, but their claws make them champion diggers, so instead of running from enemies they sometimes merely dig in. Both animals are endangered by the destruciton of their forest habitats in South America. A similar animal, the pangolin or scaly anteater, *Manis temmincki*, inhabits central Africa. Pangolins are captured and traded illegally to supply material for boots.

The Brazilian three-toed sloth, *Bradypus torquatus*, is a small, tree-dwelling mammal of Central and South America. It travels upside down and moves slowly but will quickly defend itself against attack. It eats mainly vegetation and it too is threatened by the loss of its forest habitat.

Earth's mighty oceans contain great stores of fish and other marine animals, but paradoxically they also contain many animals that should instead exist on land because they are mammals. Some of these creatures are the most beautiful, the most legendary, the largest and the most endangered on Earth.

Otters are expert swimmers and spend a great deal of time in the water for a basically land animal. They have webbed feet and use their tails as rudders; their whiskers help them find fish. Because the sea otter does not have a layer of blubber for insulation, it must spend much of its life feeding to keep warm. It is considered a "key species" important to the environment because it eats fish and invertebrates that damage kelp beds, but this also makes it an enemy of fishermen. It is also prized for its fur.

The southern sea otter, *Enhydra lutris nereis*, inhabits the entire west coast of the United States all the way down to Baja California in Mexico. The California population has dwindled from 16,000 in the 1830s to 1,700. There are about 125,000 worldwide. Fishermen continue to consider it a pest and it often drowns in their nets, along with other marine mammals. The marine otter, *Lutra felina*, found in the waters off southern Chile, is both blessed and cursed with beautiful fur, for which it is hunted. Like other marine otters, it is more riverine and coastal than seagoing. Several other species of otter inhabit waterways in South America; the giant otter, *Pteronura brasiliensis*, averages five to six feet in length and has reached seven. The Cameroon clawless otter, *Aonyx ongica microdon*, is found in that African country and Nigeria.

Seals are among the world's cutest animals, a favorite of children, and it seems outrageous that they are made to suffer such grisly forms of death as clubbing and skinning alive to satisfy the market for furs. Despite the highly visible campaigns conducted by animal-rights organizations and celebrities, the slaughter continues.

Despite its name, the Mediterranean monk seal, *M. monachus*, is also found off northwest Africa and in the Black Sea. Monk seals are declining in number; perhaps 500 remain, their hopes dependent on the establishment of reserves in Greece and Turkey. They are shy and like solitude, but seldom find it because of tourists, fishermen and hunters. Sewage and oil pollution of the seas, especially the Mediterrean, poses a serious threat to their survival. The Caribbean, *M. tropicalis*, and Hawaiian, *M. schauinslandi*, varieties are similarly endangered.

The dugong, *Dugong dugon*, a herbivorous, seal-like mammal reaching as much as 12 feet in length, has flippers and a fishlike tail. It ranges widely over the seas from East Africa and the continent's southern tip to southern Japan and northern Australia. It is hunted for its meat, hide and the oil obtained from it. Its slow reproduction rate and vulnerability make it increasingly threatened.

The manatee, a similar mammal, suckles its young sitting in an upright position. It is said that this sight, combined with fog and perhaps seaweed draped across the animals' heads, resembling hair, caused sailors of old to belive they had seen mermaids, but any such sailors undoubtedly had drunk too much rum. The manatee is shy but will sometimes respond to snorkelers. Among the hazards to the varieties of manatee are sudden drops in temperature, outboard motors, and those who slaughter them for food. The Caribbean or West Indian manatee, *Trichechus manatus*, numbers several thousand; not much is known about the West African variety, *T. senegalensis*. The South American river manatee, *T. inunguis*, is a rare freshwater variety that has not recovered from its large-scale export as a canned delicacy.

The largest animals in the world, and the most legendary, are the whales. From the biblical tale of Jonah to Herman Melville's classic novel *Moby Dick*, these giants of the sea have stirred the imagination with mystical symbolism. In recent years whale-hunting, one of the many subjects of Melville's book, has stirred intense controversy about its necessity and cruelty. Whales of all sorts have been subjected to the terror of the hunt by teams from many nations. Environmental organizations like GreenPeace have rallied around these mammals, making them a symbol. In the 1970s members challenged whaling boats by blocking their path and shielding the whales from harpoons.

Whales feed on small marine animals or by skimming large amounts of nutritious plankton from sea water. Most whales travel along a set route from feeding grounds near the poles to mating areas in the tropics. Despite an international moratorium on hunting declared in 1985, countries like the Soviet Union, Japan, Iceland, Norway, South Korea and the Philippines plot the migration courses and intercept them in their large schools. Not much is known about some species because scientific studies were pre-empted by the hunt, and too few individuals exist to conduct studies today. As the larger, more desirable species have become depleted, whalers in turn have turned to smaller varieties. Calves are often harpooned to attract their mothers.

The right whale, *Balaena glacialis*, so called because of the quantity of oil in its blubber, its ease of capture and the fact that it did not sink after being killed made it the "right" whale to hunt, was the first to become scarce. The whaling industry, itself threatened with extinciton, developed faster boats and harpoons that could be shot from guns instead of merely hurled by hand.

The bowhead whale, *B. mysticetus*, was officially protected in 1947. Only Alaskan Eskimos, the Inuit people, were allowed to hunt it since they depended on it for food, tools and other items. Their traditional hunting methods were not seen as a threat, but their techniques and equipment entered the modern age and were believed to have reduced the whale's numbers to between 600 and 2,000 by 1976. The Inuit finally agreed to return to their traditional hunting methods, after which it was discovered that the number had been underestimated. The population is no believed to be about 4,400; about 20 a year are taken, as opposed to 60 before 1978.

The blue whale, *Balaenoptera borealis,* the world's largest animal, measures almost 100 feet and weighs 150 tons. It once numbered 100,000, but only perhaps 10 percent of that number remain.

Thirty thousand sperm whales, *Physeter catodon,* were once the average annual catch; today isolated schools of 10 or fewer are the average sighting. It provides valuable products used in oil, creams and perfumes, and thus has been an unfortunate victim.

The gray whale, *Eschrichtius robustus,* almost became extinct but was recovered through 44 years of international protection. It is a popular sight on whale-watch cruises off Baja California, but it was once called the "devilfish" because it would return attacks upon it from whaling boats. Between 1840 and 1940 its numbers in the eastern Pacific were reduced from 24,000 to a few thousand, but since it was protected it has recovered to its present level of about 18,000.

The humpback whale, *Megaptera novaeangliae,* at times stays motionless in the water and at other times leaves it in mighty leaps. Each whale has its own "song" lasting a few minutes to a half-hour. Like other species it often drowns in the nets of fishermen or is the victim of ocean pollution. It moves slowly and thus is easy prey for whalers.

AMPHIBIANS, REPTILES, INSECTS and FISH

Amphibians are endangered no less than any other animals, but in far fewer numbers, mostly because of habitat destruction for highways and housing. The only species affected are several frogs, toads and salamanders.

In general, frogs are distinguished from toads by their smooth skin and long legs, used for leaping; toads have warts and shorter legs used for hopping. The frog trade is a huge business; 150 million a year are exported just from India and Bangladesh. Frogs' legs, a gourmet delicacy, is partly responsible. The elimination of frogs from their habitat allows malaria-bearing mosquitoes and crop-destroying pests to flourish, and necessitates the use of harmful pesticides. India, for one, is rethinking its policy so as to better utilize the frog population.

Salamanders face extinction because of land development, building of dams, pollution, hunting and the overzealousness of professional and biological collectors. Many salamanders have protective coloration and thus are difficult to see. They will often sacrifice a limb to a predator that grabs hold, then regenerate it. Two giant salamanders, the Chinese, *Andrias d. davidianus,* and Japanese, *A.d. japonicus,* are the largest living amphibians, measuring about six feet in length. The Texas blind salamander, *Typhlomolge rathbuni,* inhabits wells, limestone caves and underground streams in that state. Some biologists feel that it may not be endangered but is scarce only because of the difficulty of locating it in such places. It was once America's only endangered salamander but has been joined by others, including the Santa Cruz long-toed salamander, *Ambystoma macrodactylum croceum,* found in mid-coastal California.

The very word "reptile" seems to have unpleasant connotations—slimy, cold-blooded animals slithering through swamps and pouncing upon unsuspecting prey, sometimes human. They are not glamour creatures; they do not get much sympathy. In fact they are an essential part of the biosphere and play an important role in nature's system of checks and balances.

The quintessential reptile is the snake, the stuff of legend, a mystical and religious symbol, hated and feared, worshipped and eaten. The names of many snakes have even been applied derogatorily to evil humans, but snakes tend to go their own way unless disturbed and they rid the landscape of pests like mice. Boas, pythons and vipers have highly sensitive heat receptors that allow them to find their prey in the dark. The many species of snakes come in a rainbow of startling colors.

Boas are constrictors; they crush their prey by coiling around it until it suffocates. They come in many varieties in many countries. The tree boa actually has a prehensile tail, which allows it to grasp its way to the top. Besides several Caribbean boas, the endangered species include two on Round Island in the Indian Ocean (discussed below). The U.S. Fish and Wildlife Service used a "sting" operation to crack a multimillion-dollar poaching ring of more than 100 people in 1981. The species being dealt included the Jamaican boa, *Epicrates subflavus*, the San Francisco garter snake, and the Indian python.

The San Francisco garter snake, *Thamnophis sirtalis tetrataenia*, is a brightly colored orange, white and black snake that inhabits marshes. It is extremely rare because of land developments but it survives because of its adaptability. It is small, has no venom and cannot constrict, so it is limited to smaller vertebrates as prey. Pythons live in Old World rain forests and thorny scrublands. They are 20 to 30 feet long; some specimens more than 30 feet have been recorded. Like many reptiles their bone system lacks terminal points that limit growth, and they can keep growing to giant size if they survive otherwise. They kill by constriction. Larger ones eat pigs or deer, but have been known to eat leopards. The Indian python, *Python m. molurus*, is hunted for its skin, used by snake charmers, held captive in zoos and snake shows, and subjected to other suffering and indignities. The female can regulate her body temperature to help incubate eggs.

The indigo snake inhabits the southeastern United States and Central and South America. It feeds on other snakes, amphibians, birds and small mammals. The eastern indigo, *Drymarchon corais couperi*, is a bluish-black endangered species.

Whenever there are rivers and swamps there exist species of crocodilians, which include crocodiles, alligators, caimans and gavials. Because of their looks, they are fairly unpopular as animals to preserve, but they are no less deserving than the more glamorous species.

The American alligator, *Alligator mississippiensis*, has made a partial recovery and is not now considered endangered in the United States, but sheer numbers do not necessarily ensure its survival. It lives in swamps in the southeastern United States and parts of the Caribbean and is somewhat more numerous in Georgia, South Carolina and Florida. Its numbers are not exactly known, but 1 million may exist. It performs an important function in the Florida Everglades by feeding on the gar, which eats smaller fish. The holes and trails the alligator digs also support other forms of life, and its nest mounds grow into small islands supporting trees. In those trees herons and egrets breed.

Between the early 1800s and 1940, 10 million of these alligators were killed for their hides. They were subsequently protected, but a certain amount of hunting is permitted. They are also farmed for food and hides. Some people, especially in states where hunting is a large industry, have argued that crocodilians are not actually endangered and should not be considered so. However, even the animals that reproduce rapidly and frequently are hard-pressed to sustain the population, since flooding, land development and predation are common. The shooting of mothers at their nests eliminates both breeding females and, soon thereafter, the defenseless young. Some species do not breed until they are eight or 10 years old, and thus do not get the chance. These include the American crocodile, *Crocodylus acutus*, a much rarer species inhabiting the same general area as the American alligator; the rare Orinoco crocodile, *C. intermedius*, of South Americas's Orinoco River basin; and the black caiman, *Melanosuchus niger*, of the Amazon Basin.

The caiman was once taken at the rate of 20,000 per year; it is stuffed and sold as a souvenir. Today it is believed to survive only in Manu National Park in Peru. Only a few hundred Orinoco crocodiles remain, and the population is so scattered that breeding is difficult.

The young are vulnerable to predators at three stages: (1) as eggs, taken by humans and other mammals, lizards and pigs; (2) as hatchlings, taken by lizards, foxes and crows; and (3) as young in the water, taken by large fish and wading birds. The mother actively protects the eggs and the hatchlings, gathering them up in her mouth for transport or protection. Conservationists sometimes collect the egges or hatchlings to rear them to about four feet, a size that makes them large enough to defend themselves.

Alligators differ from crocodiles partially in the shape of the snout—broader in the former and pointier in the latter—and in the pattern of teeth, the croc's being exposed. Most crocodilians will eat any animal, including humans, but some, like the Nile crocodile, *C. niloticus*, prefer fish, birds or hoofed mammals that are not always easy to catch. Crocodilians do not chew; they either swallow prey whole or twist and tear off pieces that can be swallowed. They sometimes lose teeth during this process but quickly grow them back. The gavial, which has a long, slender snout, has adapted its teeth to pierce slippery fish and hold them.

Most species inhabit either fresh water or salt water; a few have adapted to both. The saltwater crocodile, *C. porosus*, is found throughout Southeast Asia, Australia, Papua New Guinea and the Pacific. Protection has allowed it to recover in Papua New Guinea. A large industry based on the animal's skin flourished there, but when the numbers declined in the 1960s because of hunting, the government stepped in to allow undisturbed breeding and to establish a farming industry. Hunters were persuaded to stock farms, which were set up in conjunction with food sources such as poultry and fish farms. In 1979 the first skins from farmed crocodiles accounted for two percent of the total exports; four years later the figure was 99 percent. In Kakadu National Park and in the tropical regions of northern Australia, crocodiles and other abundant wildlife have become major tourist attractions. Protection has seen an increase in crocodile numbers and a few tourist deaths, usually caused by ignoring camping and swimming restrictions.

Monitor lizards are believed to have evolved along the same line as snakes. There are now many differences between them but they retain the same characteristic protrusible tongue. The lizards are found around water and burrow into the soil at night. They are generally large; the Komodo Island monitor or Komodo dragon, *Varanus komodoensis*, may reach 10 feet in length and weigh more than 350 pounds, although individuals that large are not usually seen now. Humans compete with the Komodo dragon for deer and wild pigs. A few hundred are believed to remain in the wild. Other, smaller species inhabit Africa and central Asia. In India they are eaten, turned into leather, and used in fertility rites and festivals, which causes them harm even if it does not kill them.

Iguanas vary from place to place. They are found all over the world on tropical islands. They have been able to proliferate because of the lack of predators, but man has gradually stepped in to fill that void. Land iguanas, genus *Conolophus*, have suffered the same fate on the Galapagos Islands as tortoises. Humans have shot them for sport, vegetation is scarce and wild goats and introduced cats prey upon them. They are now protected. At first it was believed that their status stemmed partly from the lack of exploration of the islands; Charles Darwin had, in fact, found them common in 1835. The other factors and military occupations later combined to endanger them. The Barrington land iguana, *C. pallidus*, in particular is endangered on the island of that name, numbering a few hundred. The Fiji banded iguana, *Brachylophus fasciatus*, and crested variety, *B. vitiensis*, have long tails and can reach a yard in length. They live in trees and feed on vegetation. The destruction of their habitat endangers them, as well as the introduction of mongooses, which eat them and their eggs. Other species are endangered throughout the Caribbean.

Round Island, a small volcanic island north of Mauritius in the Indian Ocean, is a veritable case study in the adverse effects of introduction of foreign species. A century ago traders introduced goats and rabbits, which promptly set about destroying the local flora. This loss of food in turn endangered several reptiles. The two varieties of day gecko, *Phelsuma edwardnewtoni* and *P. guentheri*, need palm trees for resting places, but these have been decimated. The lack of trees has caused erosion of 75 percent of the island's soil. The two local boas, *Casarea dussumieri* and *Bolyeria multocarinata*, also depended on loose soil and leaves for their

Orangutans reproduce slowly and infant mortality is high, especially in captivity.

The animal's survival rate in captivity is not too high in general.

The forests of Borneo and Sumatra are the only places where wild orangutans now exist.

They have declined in number at an alarming rate in the twentieth century, especially since World War II.

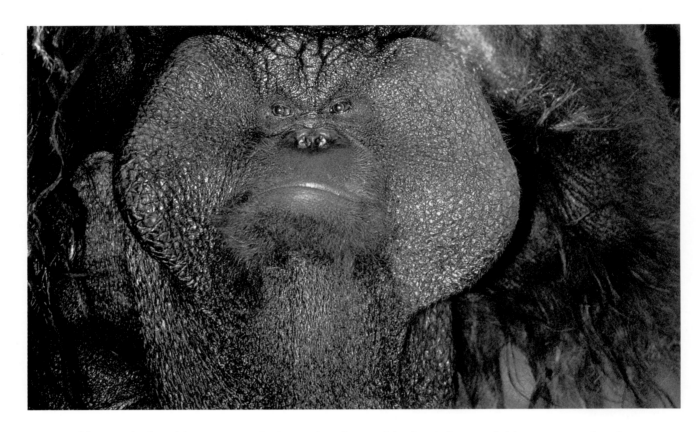

The expressive face of the orangutan makes it seem almost human. It is a favorite in zoos, television programs and movies.

The Guianan or white-faced saki mates for life and lives in a familial society.

The monogamous couple show affection toward each other and hostility toward aggressors.

Only the male of the Guianan saki has a white face. The animal has matted hair atop its head.

The mandrill of equatorial West Africa has one of the

animal kingdom's most spectacular visages. This fierce

baboon roams the savannahs and rocks in large gangs.

The gelada baboon of Ethiopia has a dark coat with a reddish chest, and a mane

around its shoulders. Its name may have come from the Arabic word for mane.

Gibraltar rock apes have inhabited that formidable redoubt for centuries and have been cared for in large part by the British Army, whose occupation of the rock is entwined by legend with that of the apes'.

The Jersey Zoo, in the United Kingdom's Channel Islands, maintains a breeding program for all gorillas in the British Isles.

The gibbon is a small ape that swings through the forests of Southeast Asia with

great speed. It lives in small, permanent families and is highly territorial.

The mountain gorilla of Rwanda has been befriended and protected by

such researchers and conservationists as George Schaller and the late Dian Fossey.

The red-face uakari lives in the forests of the Amazon Basin. Its face is a truly strange color.

The langur is a slender Asian monkey with a long tail. It dwells in trees and eats leaves.

An adult male leads a troop of about 40, and they run along the ground at high speed.

Baboons inhabit the open country of Africa and Asia in highly organized social groups.

They have powerful jaws and sharp teeth and can store food in their cheek pouches.

Some marmosets have long, tufted hair atop their ears or fur that gathers in a pompadour. Their furry tails sometimes have black or gray bands.

Goeldi's marmoset is found in Brazil, Colombia, Peru, Ecuador and Bolivia. Marmosets live in trees and eat fruits and insects.

The cotton-top marmoset is one of a group of monkeys that are the smallest ones extant. They usually get no bigger than a squirrel.

When not endangered, marmosets have been popular as pets in Central and South America. They have long, soft fur that comes in beautiful colors.

Chimpanzees are among the most popular and human-like animals. They dwell in trees and on the ground and use tools like branches and sticks to obtain insects and vegetation for food.

The pygmy chimpanzee occupies a small area of rain forest in Zaire. The destruction of the high forest it lives in is the principal threat it faces.

Macaques are short-tailed monkeys
that live in southeastern Asia,
Japan, Gibraltar and northern Africa.

The proboscis monkey is native to Borneo. The male may
have to move his nose aside to eat, but because of
its size he is also sought out by females for mating.

Troops of langurs avoid each other. They are arboreal, and the destruction
of forests for timber in such places as Sri Lanka threatens their survival.

*Like many animals, the spider monkey has not always fared well
in captivity, and efforts to induce captive breeding have been futile.*

*Even among species as agile as monkeys, spider monkeys are known as acrobats.
They use their long, prehensile tails to swing in groups through the trees of Central America.*

The red howler monkey is aptly named, for it
makes incredibly loud sounds. Early in the morning in the jungle,
distant groups announce their territory by howling.

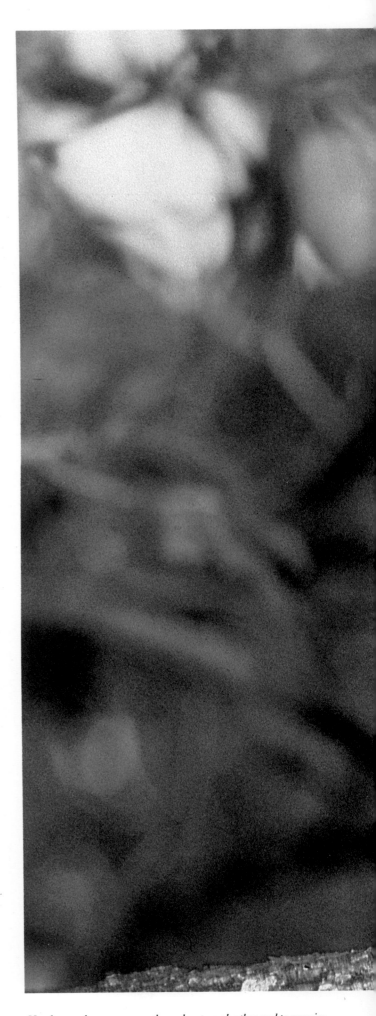

The black howler monkey is endangered throughout
its range in Mexico, Guatemala and Belize.

Howler monkeys announce themselves to each other and to enemies
with their loud cries. They can be ferocious and difficult to tame.

The sloth is a small, tree-dwelling mammal
of Central and South America. It travels
upside down and moves very slowly but
will quickly defend itself against attack.

The siamang is a large black gibbon
with an inflatable throat sac.
Siamangs are found in Malaysia and Indonesia.

The woolly monkey's main habitat is the upper Amazon Basin.

FOLLOWING PAGE:

The Bengal tiger is an excellent swimmer that sometimes takes a load off its feet after a heavy meal by relaxing in the water.

Tigers were seriously endangered throughout India because of hunting and the destruction of their habitat, but their numbers have recovered through the Project Tiger program.

The Asiatic or Indian lion has virtually disappeared. A few remain in India, but they ranged historically as far west as Turkey, Iran and Arabia.

The Florida panther, a mountain lion, is found from Louisiana and Arkansas east to South Carolina and Florida. Its eyes are adapted to night hunting, and its foot pads make it a silent stalker.

The puma goes by several names, including cougar, panther and mountain lion. Its abilities as a hunter have sometimes made it a pest to ranchers, and it has been hunted nearly to extinction itself.

The leopard is quiet and solitary, hunting mostly
at night. It eats fish and meat and thinks nothing
of tackling prey its own size. It is strong
enough to carry its kill up into a tree to eat it.

The leopard's whiskers function as antennae as
it hunts. It eats monkeys, antelopes,
jackals, peacocks and large porcupines, among
other prey, and has even been known to attack humans.

The cheetah, found from Africa to India,
outruns its prey with its sheer blinding
speed. It is the fastest four-footed animal,
exceeding 60 miles an hour for short bursts.

The beautiful jaguar exists from the southern United States into South America.

It dwells mainly in forests, but since it is not a good climber it seeks its prey on the ground.

Cheetahs and other large game animals have brought thousands

of tourists to Africa on hunting and photo safaris.

The leopard cat is about the size of a house cat
but resembles a leopard. It dwells in Southeast Asia
and its markings vary from one region to another.

The Spanish lynx is, like its close relatives,
a ferocious hunter, preying mainly on
small animals. It is found in Spain and Portugal.

The clouded leopard is small but deadly. Its fangs
are larger than any other cat's, and its raspy tongue
helps it lick the meat from the bones of its kill.

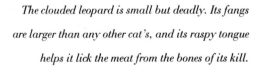

The bobcat, shown here with a serval, has shifted its habitat from its former range in central Mexico and now is scattered throughout the United States and southern Canada.

The bobcat is closely related to the lynx. It hunts rabbit, hare and sometimes deer. The hair on the soles of its feet keeps body heat in.

The ocelot inhabits the southwestern United States to Central and South America.

Its coat is decorated with spots, stripes and rings. No two cats are alike.

The snow leopard is extremely rare. The hair on the soles of its feet protects them and gives it

traction in its habitat, at elevations of 10,000 to 20,000 feet in the mountains of Asia.

Caribou migrate south to the forests in the winter and return north to the tundra

in the spring. Activities such as the construction of pipelines interrupt their route.

Woodland caribou are endangered in parts of the northwestern United States and southern Canada.

As with other animals in this area, logging activities pose the principal threat.

The walia or Abyssinian ibex lives high in the mountains and feeds on vegetation.

The sika is considered one of the most attractive members of the deer family, but it has also been one of the least protected.

Wild goats live in herds. They are also bred for their milk and wool, which provides cashmere and mohair.

The agile ibex easily negotiates the mountainous country it resides in.

FOLLOWING PAGE:

The impala can leap 10 feet into the air and 30 feet forward in one bound.

Impalas are non-territorial and live in herds of up to 60 animals.

The eland yields fine meat and leather, and therefore the measures enacted to protect it have been only sporadically enforced.

Because soldiers and government workers in Africa have used gazelles for target practice, hunting has been curtailed.

In the 1970s the Arabian oryx became extinct in the wild,

but it was reintroduced into a region of Oman by a local people.

Gazelles are two-toned as protective coloration against predators.

The chamois is a goat that makes tremendous leaps through the spectacular mountains of Europe.

The hartebeest, a relative of the gnu, is also
similar to the horse in physiology and swiftness.

A vicuña reserve in Peru has preserved the animals,
but the program was so successful that
they may have been prematurely culled.

The Peruvian government's ban on the export
of vicuña wool and the end of imports by other
countries have helped save the animal.

Other animals often eat the vegetation needed by deer, but they sometimes eat useless strains that compete for growing space.

In the mid-1970s the marsh deer was among four species identified as being at special risk. It was the subject of a special study for management and recovery.

The vicuña is valued for its soft, warm fleece. The ancient Incas sheared the animals annually, but the Spanish conquistadors merely killed and skinned t

The Rocky Mountain mule deer is found in the mountains and deserts of western North America.

The Florida Key deer, a pale deer with small antlers, lives on the Florida Keys, swimming from one island to another. It has been eliminated from several by human encroachment.

A smaller relative of the kangaroo, some species of the wallaby have struggled to survive since European settlement. Endangered species, notably the parma wallaby, have been bred in captivity and released in the wild.

Subject of controversy in international conservation circles, populations of the kangaroo are closely monitored. Species which could be endangered, such as the eastern gray and the western gray, are protected by law.

Red kangaroos at play. With an estimated two million red kangaroos in New South Wales alone, the world's largest living marsupial is under no threat of extinction.

Considered a rural pest in some area, legal culling of kangaroos remains a contentious issue with some experts suggesting they be incorporated into the pastoral industry.

The Asian elephant has smaller ears and tusks than the African variety.

The illegal hunting of elephants for the ivory of their tusks has greatly reduced their numbers.

FOLLOWING PAGE:

An elephant gestates for about two years. The young will live with the mother as part of the herd for another eight to 12 years.

Mountain tapirs are striped when they are young, but lose the stripes in adulthood. Despite their somewhat awkward appearance, they are good swimmers, fast runners and expert climbers.

The tapir spends much of its time in the water and mud of the Central American rain forest.

The elephant's trunk is a combination nose and upper lip. It is powerful enough to lift tree trunks yet sensitive enough to grasp a single fruit.

A symbolic American scene—the buffalo roams in Yellowstone National Park. It is more correctly called a wood bison.

At one time there were 60 million wood bison in the American West. The number dwindled to a few hundred a century ago, but they have made a slow recovery to several thousand.

The Bactrian camel is a staple of transportation and commerce in areas such as northern China, where it has performed its function for centuries.

Przewalski's horse is a wild horse of northern China. The harsh,

forbidding country it inhabits has helped isolate it from human encroachment.

Few wild horses exist today. Przewalski's horse is believed

to have been the ancestor of all domestic varieties.

The yak is used as a beast of burden in central Asia. Its ability

as a climber is valued in such rugged regions as Xizang (Tibet).

Nomadic herders tend flocks of yak in the Pamir Mountains of central Asia.

The few yaks that have not been hunted to extinction are used to plow the land and pull heavy loads. They are also used for their milk, meat and leather.

*Bears seldom leave their habitat and confront
humans, but when they do they often eat vegetables
or kill farm animals, which makes them unwelcome.*

*Bears are responsible for increased
public consciousness about the environment
and conservation, but the increased tourism
in their habitats sometimes taxes the land.*

*The grizzly bear can grow to $7^{1}/_{2}$ feet long
and 800 pounds. Hardly any other animal
is a match for its incredible strength;
it can break a bison's neck with one blow.*

The panda is currently engaged in a life-and-death struggle as conservationists and the Chinese government try to protect it in specially created reserves and "pandaminiums."

The giant panda is the symbol of the World Wildlife Fund because it is cute, cuddly and one of the rapidly shrinking species on the endangered list.

The white rhinoceros inhabits central Africa. It may have been exterminated in certain areas and then reintroduced from others.

The hippopotamus, which is largely aquatic, eats reeds and other vegetation that would otherwise clog waterways. It easily walks on the bottom of rivers.

The black rhino of sub-Saharan Africa. Rhinos are unlawfully slaughtered for their horns, which are made into dagger handles and are reputed to have medicinal powers.

FOLLOWING PAGE:

The only mountain zebras left live in reserves, but even there they face danger from hunters, as well as disease.

There are several varieties of kit fox, but the San Joaquin variety, found in California, faces the greatest danger.

Wolves are nocturnal hunters, often traveling 40 to 50 miles a night in pursuit of quarry. They have a highly developed social system and usually mate for life.

The swift fox inhabits Canada and the northern plains of the United States. It eats mice, small mammals, insects and fruit.

Folklore has done much to fan the flames of primal

fear about wolves, which have traditionally suffered

both image problems and hysterical persecution.

The hyena is a scavenger that roams at night. It is distinguished by its cry, which sounds like strange laughter.

Hyenas use their strong jaws to crush bones. They feed on carrion littering the plains of Africa and Asia.

The carnivorous hyena has coarse hair and short back legs.

The beaver is a highly social rodent. The dams built by beaver communities create necessary ponds and pastures, and the animals' threatened extinction also threatens these areas.

The small, mouse-like chincilla was once common in the Andes but was hunted to near extinction for its thick coat.

Kangaroo rats are small, leaping rodents that live in the deserts of North America. They are also called pocket rats because they carry food in their cheek pouches.

Patagonian cavies were once called pampas hares because of their resemblance to that animal. They are good at running, jumping and digging.

Rodents are the most proliferous mammals, comprising more than half of all species. Their unpopularity stems from their perceived role as disease carriers.

Probably the most well-known and fascinating of Madagascar's endangered species are the approximately 40 types of lemurs.

Lemurs are intelligent arboreal primates that have soft fur, long tails, long snouts and large bug-eyes.

Wolves, eagles and bears are among the marmot's enemies. Its vision and

hearing are keen, and it makes several different sounds to express its emotional state.

Prairie dogs live in ``towns,'' some of which have been known to extend

for 100 miles and include millions of the highly social animals.

Marmots hibernate in the winter, and mate as soon as they come out. Some remain near the den year-round; others travel far afield.

Otters are expert swimmers and spend a great deal of time in the water,

especially for a land animal. They have webbed feet and use their tails as rudders.

Because the sea otter, unlike the seals, does not have a layer of blubber

to insulate it, it must spend much of its life feeding to keep warm.

Monk seals are declining in number. They are shy and like solitude,

but seldom find it because of tourists and fishermen.

Seals are making a comeback on the Galapagos Islands. They coexist peacefully with other marine life such as crabs and iguanas.

Despite its name, the Mediterranean monk seal is also found off northwest Africa and in the Black Sea.

Among the hazards to the several varieties of manatee are sudden drops in temperature, outboard motors and those who slaughter them for food.

FOLLOWING PAGE:

Iguanas have bene able to proliferate because of the lack of predators, but man has gradually stepped in to fill that void.

119

Pangolins are captured and traded illegally to supply material for boots.

Iguanas have suffered the same fate on the Galapagos Islands as tortoises.

Humans, introduced cats and lack of vegetation have endangered them.

Iguanas vary from place to place. They are found

all over the world on tropical islands.

The crocodile's appearance has made it fairly
unpopular as an animal to preserve, but it is no
less deserving than the more glamorous species.

The American alligator has made a partial recovery,
but it is still endangered or threatened. It lives
in swamps in the southeastern United States.

Salamanders face extinction because of land
development, building of dams, pollution and the
overzealousness of professional and biological collectors.

Many salamanders have protective
coloration and thus are difficult to see.
They will often sacrifice a limb to a
predator that grabs hold, then regenerate it.

The Galapagos tortoise was part
of the solution to the origin of
species first postulated by Charles Darwin
during a voyage on the Pacific Ocean.

Early ship captains found the Galapagos
Islands unattractive and inhospitable,
but seamen quickly began to exterminate
the local tortoise for its meat.

The indigo snake inhabits the southeastern United States and Central and

South America. It feeds on other snakes, amphibians, birds and small mammals.

Pythons live in Old World rain forests and thorny scrublands.

Larger ones eat pigs or deer, and have even been known to eat leopards.

Boas come in many varieties in many countries. The tree boa actually

has a prehensile tail, which allows it to grasp its way to the top.

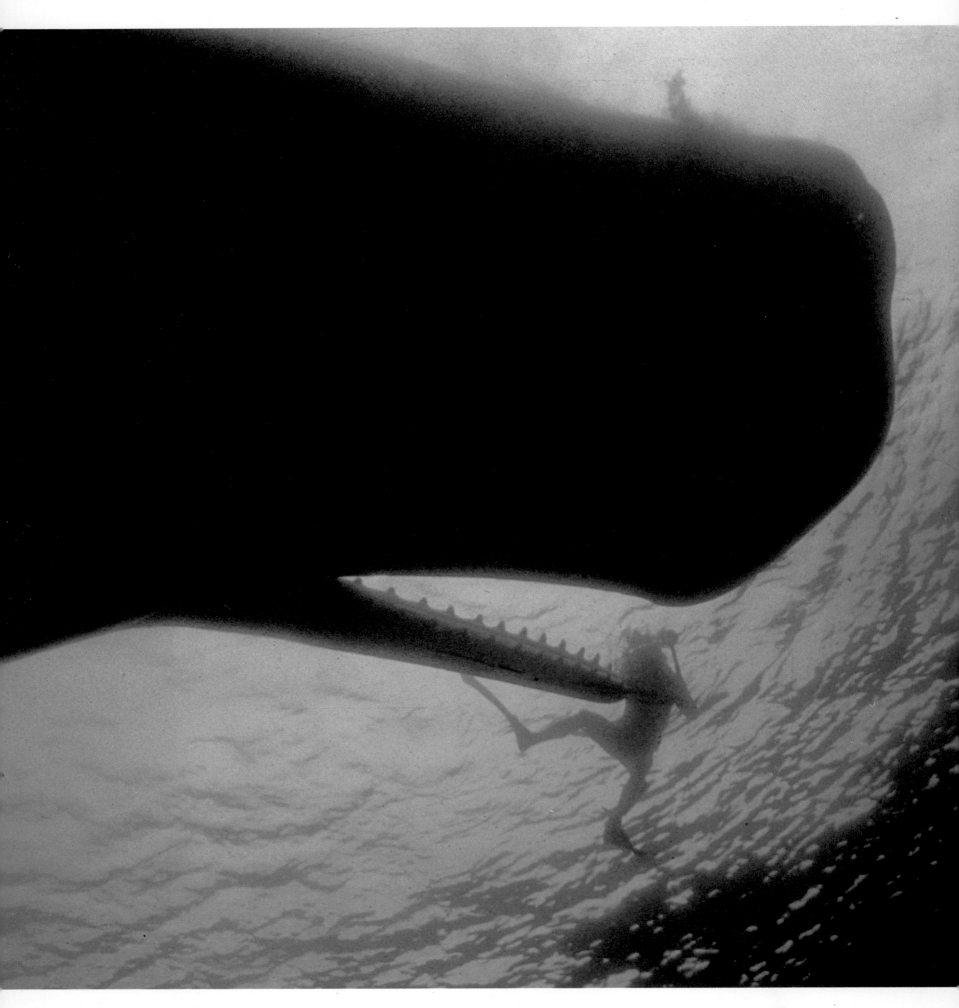

Whales of all sorts have been subjected to the terror of the hunt by teams from many

nations. Environmental organizations have rallied around these mammals, making them a symbol.

*The gray whale almost became extinct but was recovered through 44 years of
international protection. It is a popular sight on whale-watch cruises off Baja California.*

*The humpback whale travels along a set route from
feeding grounds near the poles to mating areas in the tropics.*

The brown pelican differs from other species by the color of its plumage.
It dives into the water to gather fish into its bill and pouch.

Albatrosses use the wind to help them take off. They glide to
a landing on water to feed on several varieties of marine life.

The whooping crane, shown here with sandhill cranes,
once flourished in marshlands and bogs, but the
development of cities and croplands altered its habitat.

The Galapagos hawk is extremely rare.
The islands' early settlers routinely
clubbed it to death to protect their poultry.

The bald eagle, the symbol of America, has had a confused reputation ever
since Benjamin Franklin accused it of being a coward. It is actually a fearless hunter.

Some kites are scavengers, while others are effective hunters.
They swoop down suddenly on their prey, whether it is dead or alive.

Rampant collecting and forest-clearing threaten the Philippine
monkey-eating eagle. Its head feathers and bill make it a dramatic-looking bird.

FOLLOWING PAGE:

The ostrich has adapted for life in the desert.
Ostrich farms have also been established to ensure both
its survival and a good supply of plumes and leather.

The beautiful hyacinth macaw of the South American rain forest can break open a Brazil nut with its powerful bill.

Parrots are talkative and prized as pets. A brisk international

trade exists in these birds, many of which die because of poor handling.

Several small owls known as Scops owls inhabit the South Pacific and Southeast Asia. They rarely build nests, preferring to use hollowed-out trees.

The predatory sparrowhawk uses its great flying ability to maneuver through the forest and take smaller birds right out of the air.

The American bobwhite lays 12 to 24 eggs at one time.

The bustard is a terrestrial bird that is good at running. It goes into elaborate flight and inflates a gular pouch during courtship.

A few species of woodpeckers have actually benefited from forest clearance because they prefer dead trees.

The ungainly booby is better in flight than on land. It glides easily and can sleep on the water.

Cranes eat a great deal of
animals, insects and vegetation.
This sandhill crane is nibbling
grass in a Florida marsh.

burrows. The Round Island kink, *Leiolopisma telfairi,* has also been severely affected. Conservationists have removed the goats but the rabbits remain; the regeneration of plant life will not occur until they leave.

Tortoises and turtles have increasingly been hunted to near extinction for leather and food, and the beaches on which they breed have been overdeveloped or overrun by collectors and hunters. Some tortoises have been known to survive for as many as 200 years, turtles for somewhat less time.

Early ship captains found the Galapagos Islands unattractive and inhospitable, but seamen quickly began to exterminate the local tortoise for its meat. The Galapagos giant tortoise, *Geochelone elphantopus,* the world's largest, weighs more than 500 pounds and provided plenty of food. More than 15,000 were taken between 1811 and 1844. The practice continued until they could not be found. Introduced goats also competed with them for vegetation. The tortoises still inhabit the numerous islands and are occasionally spotted in various stages of growth. Some islands contain only a few individuals, others hundreds. Captive breeding programs aim to restore their numbers; some species cannot raise young effectively because of predation upon the eggs by rats, dogs and pigs.

The loggerhead turtle, *C. caretta,* has a hard, bony shell that is sought for trade. It eats many varieties of fish and therefore competes with fishermen. It is collected as food and for its shell and sometimes becomes entangled and dies in nets. Both it and the green turtle, *Chelonia mydas,* are circumglobal; they swim the tropical and temperate seas and oceans in search of shellfish and crustaceans. Breeding colonies have been established in Florida and on Mexico's Pacific Coast. The green turtle, believed to number several thousand, has been found to migrate to the same nests for breeding every two to three years. Both species are adversely affected by interference with these beaches. Raccoons and other predators eat the eggs and the lights from developments near the beaches draw the turtles inland, where they are run over on highways or die in the broiling sun.

The hawksbill sea turtle, *Eretmochelys imbricata,* which inhabits tropical seas, was the beneficiary of a plastic imitation of its shell, which seemed to satisfy souvenir hunters in the 1950s in Costa Rica, one of its breeding sites. But 10 years later collectors resumed their quest for the genuine article, the leather market sought its skin, and the gourmet food trade turned its meat into soup. These incentives caused hunters to ignore any threat of extinction. Likewise, 40,000 females of Kemp's Ridley sea turtle, also called the Atlantic Ridley sea turtle, *Lepidochelys kempii,* gathered to breed on a Mexican beach in the early 1950s. By 1967 the number, probably representing most of the world population, had dropped to 2,200, and most of the eggs they laid were stolen by poachers.

Fish tend to be thought of more as food than as endangered species, but they suffer no less than other animals from predation or when their habitats are destroyed. Part of the lack of public consciousness is the fact that fish inhabit another medium, water, and are not easily seen except in aquariums, so they tend to be forgotten. Perhaps more than other animals, many fish become extinct before they are even discovered, spending their entire existence in the depths of the ocean. Information is not available even on many known species because of the difficulty in studying them. The increasing human population, industrialization, development of land and water and pollution greatly affect fish, which cannot escape to another enviroment and may not even have another location to flee to.

The Leon Springs pupfish, *Cyprinodon bovinus,* found near Fort Stockton, Texas, is not believed to have been seen since it was first described in 1851, despite repeated efforts. It may have become extinct because of disturbance of its habitat and the introdution of exotics. A more famous species, the Devil's Hole pupfish, *C. diabolis,* is restricted to a single spring-fed pool in the Ash Meadows oasis near Death Valley in Nevada. It seems to be resistant to any type of cultivation. When ground water was pumped out by a nearby agricultural operation, endangering the fish, the Supreme Court decided on a minimum water level and the oasis subsequently became a wildlife refuge.

The three-inch-long snail darter, *Percina tanasi,* was involved in one of the most famous court battles in conservation history. In the late 1960s the Tennessee Valley Authority planned a $120 million development that included the Tellico Dam in a Little Tennessee River valley. The dam would provide hydroelectric power and control floods, but the area was lived in and used for recreation and fishing and contained an important

Cherokee archeological site. The local people were upset and sued. A required environmental impact statement was filed and noted several rare fishes in the river.

While the project was on hold, Congress passed the 1973 Endangered Species Act, whose purpose was to prevent species from becoming extinct because of human intervention and to preserve the environment. At about the same time, a biologist discovered the previously unknown snail darter, a perch that feeds on snails, in the river. Its habitat would be destroyed by the dam project, which was by then proceeding. The TVA fought to keep the snail darter off the endangered species list and lost, attempted unsuccessfully to move the fish to other waterways, and pressed ahead with the project—the result being further and more complex litigation. The Supreme Court ruled against the dam in 1978, the same year the act was due to expire. The dam was eventually shown to be a financial boondoggle, but an Act of Congress allowed it finally to be built, exempt from compliance with not only this act but with all others that could have stopped it, such as the Historic Preservation and Clean Water acts.

BIRDS

There are about 8,600 species of birds, and a relatively small number are endangered. One might then ask, Why be concerned? The reason is that birds occupy an important niche in the enviroment. Some are predators, some provide food and some eliminate insects and other pests. Without them the fragile ecosystem would quickly collapse. What follows is a description of some of the more well-known endangered species.

The order *Falconiformes* comprises several diurnal birds of prey like hawks, eagles and falcons. Among them are such well-known species as the California condor and the bald eagle.

The California condor, *Gymnogyps californianus*, is one of the world's largest and heaviest flying birds, more than 25 pounds and five feet from head to tail. Habitat destruction and hunting endanger it, and scientists are trying to save it from extinction through captive breeding. In 1988 only 27 remained, all in zoos, and they were not on display; they are extinct in the wild. The condor normally feeds on carrion but does not hunt living animals. Its flight is a memorable sight. If the wind is right it can glide high in the sky for more than 10 miles without have to move its huge wings. One measure used in reserves is the establishment of "vulture restaurants" in which the entrails and bones of animals are put out specifically to feed vultures.

The sparrow hawk uses its great flying ability to maneuver through the forest and take smaller birds right out of the air. The name comes from its smaller size, not what it eats, which is insects, small mammals and other birds. The Anjouan Island species, *Accipiter francessi pusillus*, is endangered in its habitat on the Comoro Islands in the Indian Ocean.

The Galapagos hawk, *Buteo galapagoensis*, is extremely rare. The islands' early settlers routinely clubbed it to death to protect their poultry. Because of the remote environment of those islands the hawks, like other animals, were remarkably tame and trusting of man, which led to their downfall.

Some kites are scavengers, while others are effective hunters. They swoop down suddenly on their prey, whether it is dead or alive. The Everglade snail kite, *Rostrhamus sociabilis plumbeus*, is a hawk with an elongated upper bill and an unusual method of feeding. It flies over Florida waterways looking for large snails. When it finds one it swoops down and grasps the snail with one foot, takes it to a perch and waits for it to emerge from its shell. When it does the kite impales it on its sharp bill and severs it from the shell. The development of the landscpe not only endangers the kite but also disrupts its food source. Conservationists have stocked the waters with snails in an attempt to attract and feed kites.

Eagles have a regal, imperious look. With their sharply focused eyes, hooked bill and large talons, they seem to challenge any and all comers. They are indeed lords among birds, but they face grave threats to their survival.

The bald eagle, *Haliaeetus leucocephalus*, the symbol of America, has had a confused reputation ever since

Benjamin Franklin accused it of being a coward, but it is actually a fearless hunter. It has traditionally ranged throughout North America but is endangered almost everywhere except in a few northwestern states, where it is threatened. Only in Alaska does it exist in large numbers; thousands can be seen in autumn feeding on salmon on the rivers. Its habitat is being encroached upon and polluted and the eagle itself is hunted, albeit illegally. More than 100,000 were shot in Alaska alone between 1915 and 1951. DDT and other insecticides also affect it through the fish it eats, not necessarily causing death but ruining eggs that are subsequently laid. DDT is no longer used but it may remain in the environment for years.

Bald eagles can subsist on carrion, especially when young and inexperienced at hunting. They normally feed on fish, whales, seals, smaller mammals like sea otters and other birds. They can enter the water to obtain fish when necessary. They will hunt from a perch, from the air or in flight, and will even steal the catches of other animals. In the 1970s a breeding station was established on Amchitka in the Aleutian Islands and 50 nesting pairs of birds were able to feed at a nearby garbage dump. But the numbers of young decreased 70 percent when the human population left and the dump closed. It is slow to breed and one sibling often kills another in competition for food. A solution is for conservationists to rear them apart and return the young to the nest at a later date.

More than 1,000 pairs live in the contiguous 48 states, and thousands more migrate from the north in winter. The U.S. Fish and Wildlife Service is conducting a recovery program to save the eagle, one of the more popular species in the conservation movement.

The white-tailed eagle, *H. albicilla*, is Europe's largest, more than three feet from bill to tail. It was common in the early nineteenth century until it was suspected of attacks on sheep and became the target of hunters and collectors. It started to recover from near extinction after World War II but then became the victim of more hunting, habitat destruction, pesticides and the poisons put out for foxes and ravens. Between 50 and 80 pairs of the Greenland variety remain; in other countries the number may be lower. A program has begun to reintroduce the eagle into Scotland. One method that helps it and other birds breed successfully is a round-the-clock vigil by volunteers, sometimes drawn from the lay community.

The harpy eagle, *Harpia harpyja*, found from Mexico to Argentina, is considered the most powerful. It preys on all other birds and many mammals and does not fear to tackle such animals as monkeys or porcupines. It has distinctive head feathers and immense talons, which it uses in flight to snatch animals clinging tightly to trees. Its major nemesis is habitat destruction.

Rampant collecting and forest-clearing threaten the Philippine monkey-eating eagle, *Pithecophaga jefferyi*. Its head feathers and bill make it a dramatic-looking bird. Despite its name it also takes deer, other birds and snakes, flying high above the trees, then swooping down to attack. Studies backed by the World Wildlife Fund are under way to protect both the eagle and its habitat and to learn more about them, but as in so many cases such studies are put on hold in times of civil unrest. There may be a few hundred in existence.

The Spanish imperial eagle, *Aquila heliaca adalberti*, unlike many eagles, does not usually choose mountains for its aerie, preferring woods and grasslands. As such, it encounters man more often and suffers the consequences of his persecution and pollution. It eats small mammals. About 60 pairs survive in Spain.

There are 17 races of peregrine falcons, *Falco peregrinus*, ranging throughout the world. They are the supreme species in falconry because of their fast, accurate flight and deadly hunting skills. They can swoop and turn at high speed and dive vertically onto other birds for the kill. Insecticides ingested by their prey species are killing off falcons. They inhabit the Northern Hemisphere and the Arctic and migrate to South Ameria, Africa and the Middle East in winter. In the early 1980s the U.S. Fish and Wildlife Service ran a three-year undercover investigation called Operation Falcon. It brought to justice many worldwide smugglers but the black market may still be operating.

Kestrels are also falcons inhabiting various places, including Mauritius and the Seychelles in the Indian Ocean. The rare Mauritus kestrel, *F. punctatus*, feeds on geckos, which in turn feed on insects. When the native flora is destroyed by introduced species, the insects decline, and thus so do the geckos and kestrels. Management programs have concentrated on getting enough geckos to the kestrels during the breeding season. The birds do not fare well in captivity, and in the wild their nests are raided by monkeys. A few dozen kestrels are all that remain. Mauritius parakeets, *Psittacula echo*, similarly low in numbers, face the same problem, and boxes have been set up to protect the nests.

Owls are generally nocturnal birds of prey. They have come to symbolize wisdom, perhaps because of their stoic countenance. They hunt small birds, insects, small mammals and fish. Morden's owlet, *Otus ireneae*, is a Scops owl that inhabits what is left of the Sokoke forest in coastal Kenya. Bird collectors and forest clearance have made it rare. The Seychelles owl, *O. insularis*, was believed to be extinct but individuals were found in 1959 in a remote mountain area. Very little is known about it even today. Others in the small Scops species inhabit the South pacific and Southeast Asia. They rarely build nests, preferring to use hollowed-out trees. A larger species, the giant Scops, *O. gurneyi*, about a foot from head to tail, inhabits the Philippines.

Parrots are talkative and prized as pets. A brisk international trade exists in these birds, many of which die because of poor handling. Moving the birds, exporting and re-exporting them, sometimes keeps officials confused as to the numbers and destinations. Between May 1980 and August 1981 more than 33,000 birds went through Amsterdam, once a major hub for this trade, but in 1984 the Netherlands joined the Convention on Trade in Endangered Species, which attempts to regulate or at least monitor it. India, Singapore, Peru and Tanzania are among the biggest exporters. About 1 million parrots are traded every year; estimates are that the 10,000 that enter the United States are a mere fraction of the number that do not survive capture or the trip. Several species in the Caribberan, especially on St. Lucia, St. Vincent and Puerto Rico, and in Brazil have been the victims of collectors, habitat destruction and introduced rodents that prey on their eggs and young.

The short-tailed albatross, *Diomedea albatrus*, found throughout the North Pacific, uses the wind to help it take off. It glides to a landing on water to feed on several varieties of marine life. It has a wingspan of about seven feet; the largest albatross wingspan is almost 12 feet. Hurricanes and volcanoes have destroyed its nests and hunters have sought its feathers. A half-million were taken on Japanese islands between 1887 and 1903; by 1933 only 100 remained.

The ungainly booby is better in flight than on land. It glides easily and can sleep on the water. Abbott's booby, *Sula abbotti*, inhabits Christmas Island in the Indian Ocean.

The brown pelican, *Pelecanus occidentalis*, found from the southern United States to South America, differs from other species by the color of its plumage. It dives into the water to gather fish into its bill and distensible pouch. It then drains out the water and swallows the fish. Pesticides in the waters of its habitat cause it to lay thin-shelled eggs, which break when it tries to incubate them.

Cahows, *Pterodroma cahow*, inhabit the North Atlantic and Bermuda. Similar to the extinct dodo in that they were flavorful and easy to kill, they almost suffered the same fate. In the mid-seventeenth century they were gobbled up by seamen, who finished them off when famine struck. In the twentieth century they started to show up again, and in 1951 seven pairs were found in the area. Chicks were killed by rats and other birds took over the nests, disposing of the eggs. The nest burrows were modified to deny entrance to other species, and more cahows were discovered on nearby islands. DDT then became a problem. The cahow bravely prevailed, however, and now numbers about 100, shattering the belief that it was "dead as a dodo."

The Galapagos penguin, *Spheniscus mendiculus*, inhabits the cool coastal waters off those islands. It is the rarest penguin and an unusual one, located as it is so close to the Equator.

Cranes stretch out their necks and legs in flight, flapping their wings slowly and gracefully. They are good fliers but spend a good deal of time on the ground. They are highly social. They eat a great deal of both animals and vegetation. The sandhill crane, *Grus canadensis*, breeds in colder climes of northern Canada and the United States, but winters farther south. The whooping crane, *G. americana*, the tallest American bird at 4.5 feet, once flourished in marshlands and bogs, but the development of cities and croplands altered its habitat. It has been fighting extinction since the 1930s. Only in 1954 was its nesting ground discovered in a remote area of Canada, and biologists began a program to save it.

Its migration route to its winter base on the Gulf Coast of Texas was protected, farmers and hunters being educated about its plight along the way. Two eggs are laid but normally only one chick survives, so the extra eggs were incubated at a research center in Maryland. When those chicks grew to maturity and bred, the eggs were transplanted to sandhill cranes' nests in Idaho, where they were successfully raised. A new migration route was also established as insurance in case something happened to the other flock. About 100 whoopers remain.

The Chinese egret, *Egretta eulophotes*, sought for its plumes, had already disappeared from some areas of China and Korea by the time scientists got around to exploring for and studying it in the nineteenth century. Not much information is available about it, although a few small breeding populations are thought to remain in the Korean peninsula and southern China.

The wood stork, *Mycteria americana*, which shares the same habitat as the Everglade kite, is subject to the same pressures of that environment. Its nests are threatened by drought and frost, during which it may wander far afield in search of more acceptable conditions. It is the only stork that breeds in North America.

The ostrich, *Struthio camelus*, has adapted for the life and heat of the deserts of North African and Saudi Arabia. Ostrich farms have also been established to ensure both its survival and a good supply of plumes and leather. It lays up to 20 large eggs weighing three pounds each. It can run as fast as 40 mph in 15-foot strides, outstripping predators.

The bustard is a terrestrial bird that is good at running. It goes into elaborate flight and inflates a gular pouch during courtship. The great Indian bustard, *Choriotis nigriceps*, is endangered because of decreasing space in its Indian and Pakistani habitats and because its size (40 pounds) makes it desirable as food.

The masked bobwhite, *Colinus virginianus ridgwayi*, a quail, is a popular game bird. It was once well known in Sonora, Mexico, and Arizona, from which it was exterminated by about 1912. Attempts at reintroduction have not been greatly successful.

Mallards, like other ducks, are sought for their flesh, feathers and eggs. Wood ducks were almost exterminated for their meat and feathers, which are made into fishing flies. Ducks in general face decreasing wetland habitats and are declining in number in North America. The 1985 population of 31 million was the lowest in 30 years; by spring 1987 it has increased only 4 million, with some species still declining. A major problem for ducks (and other birds) is the ingestion of hunters' spent lead shot, which poisons them at the rate of possibly 2 million a year. A ban on lead shot is set to take effect in 1991.

Many birds build nests on islets to protect against predators, but one species of coot builds its own island. The Hawaiian coot, *Fulica americana alai*, a ducklike species, moves well in the water and on land.

The Hawaiian duck or koloa, *Anas wyvilliana*, was part of a World Wildlfe Fund-assisted recovery program. Besides maintaining the stocks located on the islands, conservationists sent small groups to zoos and game parks around the world, then returned the captive-bred birds to the islands.

Captive breeding helped recover the Hawaiian goose or nene, *Nesochen sandvicensis*. Predators had included dogs, mongooses and humans. In 1950 the world population stood at fewer than 50, only half of them wild. Captive breeding today has multiplied their numbers several times.

The dusky seaside sparrow, *Ammospiza nigrescens*, seems to have been another metaphor. It inhabited coastal Florida in a most unusual environment: the marshes around Cape Canaveral. It was able to build up its population because this high-security area was not frequented by humans and remained largely undeveloped. But the land was later drained for purposes related to the space center and its high-tech birds, changing the environment and making it unsuitable for real ones. The number of sparrows diminished, and in June 1987 the last know pure sparrow was found dead in its cage; only hybrids remain.

What, then, will become of the animals? Their plight is often likened to that of the animals on Noah's Ark, but a better analogy might be one of an ark with a hole in it, sinking slowly. The more water it takes on, the faster it sinks. The situation is not hopeless; not yet. But clearly something must be done. The many wildlife and environmental organizations around the world are working feverishly to patch that hole, and the average person can help by supporting their work and urging legislators to pass measures to protect animals. The work is aided in small measures, too, by avoiding actions that pollute or damage the environment in small, almost unnoticeable ways. These have a way of adding up. In the end the animals of the world will not be saved because of the grand plan of one person or group, but because every person cares.

INDEX OF PHOTOGRAPHERS

Index